The Parent's Guide to Eating Disorders

What Parents Need to Know

To my three wonderful daughters

The Parent's Guide to Eating Disorders

What Parents Need to Know

Jane Smith

LION

A Lion Book
an imprint of
Lion Hudson plc
Wilkinson House, Jordan Hill Road,
Oxford OX2 8DR, England
www.lionhudson.com

ISBN 978 0 7459 5544 5

Distributed by:
UK: Marston Book Services, PO Box 269, Abingdon, Oxon, OX14 4YN

First edition 2011
10 9 8 7 6 5 4 3 2 1 0

Typeset in Adobe Caslon Pro 11/13 and Univers 55 9.5/13
Printed in Great Britain by Clays Ltd, St Ives plc

Contents

Acknowledgments

I'd like to thank all the parent contributors who have made this book one of such personal insight by being so willing to share their stories and recall their emotions. I'm very grateful to Rob Parsons, Mark Molden, and Sheron Rice, and all the staff at Care for the Family for their support – and to the staff, trustees, and medical advisors at ABC, notably Dr Dee Dawson, Jackie Disbury, and Nicola Rance. I couldn't have done without the support, advice, and good practice of Dr Matthew Dolman and Dr Ros King. Many thanks also go to David Moloney, Kate Kirkpatrick, Miranda Lever, Jessica Tinker, and Leisa Nugent at Lion Hudson for their wisdom and expertise.

Foreword

I have no doubt at all that having a child with an eating disorder is one of the most frightening and traumatic experiences a parent can go through. Often parents don't know how to begin to deal with the situation or where to turn for help or advice. That's why I count it a privilege to write the foreword to *The Parent's Guide to Eating Disorders* as it offers much-needed encouragement, hope, and advice to parents in this situation. In fact, it will be a help to anyone who is concerned for somebody they love who is suffering with this illness – husbands, wives, brothers, sisters, friends.

Jane Smith is the Director of Anorexia and Bulimia Care (ABC), one of two national organizations caring for those with eating disorders. The expertise and understanding she has gained through her years of advising and supporting parents is evident throughout this book. But it is not just a book written by "the experts"; Jane writes with the heart and compassion of a mother who has herself experienced the challenge and pain of seeing two of her own daughters through anorexia and bulimia, and also from the experience she has gained over the years working at the helpline.

Since Care for the Family began over twenty years ago, the number of calls we receive from parents of children with an eating disorder has spiralled. I believe it is vital for these parents to know that they are not alone and I am thrilled that just recently we were able to join forces with ABC to establish a telephone befriending service for parents. This service will allow parents to speak, in confidence, to another parent who has had a similar experience. It is not counselling, but an opportunity to share your story and be supported on a regular basis by someone who truly understands what you are going through.

Eating disorders can't be "cured" overnight – indeed, the road to healing is often long and hard. And that's why this book was written. *The Parent's Guide to Eating Disorders* offers parents understanding, practical suggestions, guidance, and real hope as they support those they love along that road to a better future.

Rob Parsons
Chairman and Founder of Care for the Family

About ABC's Parent Helpline

ABC is a UK organization that has been helping people with eating disorders and related self-harm for more than twenty years. I joined ABC in 2004 in order to run their parent helpline, and since then it has received calls from thousands of parents who have been loving and supporting their children of varying ages through an eating disorder. Parents phone at various stages: at the outset of the illness; in the days of suspicion and worry beforehand; through the wait for treatment; or through treatment itself towards recovery. When they call, parents are looking for advice, comfort, and encouragement from people who have been where they are now, and who really understand from their own experience what the caller is going through. The recent establishment of our Befriending Service with Care for the Family enables us to offer even greater on-going support.

The parents who call our helpline want to speak to people who are prepared to listen to their situation and answer their questions. Often they are deeply distressed, worried, and worn out. Most express feelings of being alone and of hopelessness, and have a sense of being unsupported. They want information about what they can expect from their child's illness or from treatment from the NHS, or they want to know about counselling therapy (about the different types of individual therapy available and about group and family therapy).[1]

Whatever their different needs, they all desperately want to share their story, to talk about how they are responding to their child's and family's needs, and to discuss methods they can try to prevent any further harm happening to their son or daughter. Being informed and having suggestions gives hope, and our parents' and carers' helpline offers ongoing help and hope to anyone who needs it. We hear from mothers and fathers, stepmothers and stepfathers; from brothers, sisters, aunties, grandmas, friends, girlfriends, boyfriends, and teachers who all want to help their particular sufferer.

Some mums and dads are single parents and are trying to cope alone. Some of our callers have their own health problems – sometimes serious ones – or are already supporting someone in the family with a major illness or disability as well as trying to cope with their child's eating disorder. Sometimes the child with the eating disorder also has additional needs: they may be deaf, for example, or have autism spectrum disorders (ASDs), or else suffer with another long-term illness or condition.

We hear from parents of children aged eleven, twelve, and even younger, as well as teenagers. Many are trying to support an adult son or daughter, which in itself produces specific difficulties as they are often excluded from their child's illness and therefore from any treatment. Irrespective of their different circumstances, all the parents want to understand and to help their children through the terrible ordeal towards full recovery, as well as to find a little relief from the overwhelming fear, sadness, and isolation that they experience.

Introduction

This is a book written *for* parents *by* parents in order to help you as much as possible as you support someone you love through an eating disorder and into recovery. It aims to give you some practical tips and strategies as well as insight and information, and also to reassure you that you are not alone.

During my time working at ABC's parent helpline, I have received calls from across the UK – and also from abroad – from people in all walks of life: mums and dads at home and mums and dads at work; parents who are social workers, educational psychologists, teachers, doctors, vicars, nurses, and counsellors as well as those in business. Some of them have willingly offered their experiences in answer to the questions posed in this book. These questions constitute some of those most frequently asked at ABC, although, of course, it is not possible to include everything. Although your experience may not fit exactly with the scenarios that our parents have outlined, I would encourage you to read all the questions and answers in each chapter because there is a wealth of information and experience contained in them, giving good tips and suggestions that you may be able to apply to your situation.

Each chapter also records the emotions and feelings of parents with whom we have spoken and with which you'll be able to identify. You may find it helpful to share this book with a friend, partner, or other family member, or even with a counsellor. In the parents' answers you will hear how mums and dads explain what they faced, how they felt, and what they did – and I also add my own recollections in each chapter. The short Did You Know? sections will provide you with some helpful facts; the Check Points plus suggested Action Plans for the various stages are also there to guide you.

Parents in this book have seen very good outcomes and I hope this knowledge will really encourage you. If you are worried by reading the different chapter headings in this book, or anxious that you might be upset or discouraged if you read those chapters, then I would like to reassure you that not everyone struggling with an eating disorder has to go through all the stages of the illness or treatment. And even if that does occur, full recovery from an eating disorder really is possible.

I know this because my two daughters needed to receive all the different stages of treatment for their eating disorders. They were helped by outpatient care, the local NHS Adolescent Eating Disorders Unit, general hospitals, and specialized eating disorder clinics. As a family we have been through a range of counselling options, including different types of individual psychotherapy as well as family therapy. As a mum I have experienced my daughters' life-threatening anorexia, bulimia, and self-harming, but I can also bear witness to complete recovery in my family, despite the very painful journey towards it and the length of time it involved. So I offer you my personal encouragement and also my sincere hope that this book will help you.

In thanking the parents who have contributed their stories, I would also like to thank and give recognition to the thousands of parents I have spoken to over the years: for the steadfast love they have shown their children, the heartache they have experienced, the challenges they have faced and the battles they have fought. It is to their courage and devotion, and the lives they have saved, that ABC dedicates this book.

Jane Smith
Director
Anorexia and Bulimia Care

CHAPTER 1

Suspecting Your Child Has an Eating Disorder

As parents, we are usually the first to notice when something is affecting our child and when they are behaving differently. Maybe you've bought this book because you've seen changes in your child and their behaviour around food – or perhaps you've heard them voice their concerns about their body or about how they see themselves and you're starting to get worried. Perhaps you know that your child is struggling with schoolwork, or friendships, or, if they are adult, that they are facing pressure from a demanding job, for example, or experiencing relationship difficulties. You might have noticed them losing weight, losing their appetite, or eating unusually but don't know if you should question them about it. Perhaps you've tried to question them and you've been told, "Everything's fine. Please just stop going on about it and leave me alone."

These were my daughters' responses during the early stages and, like many parents, I hoped it would be just a passing phase. But I soon began to suspect that this "phase" was developing into something far more worrying. You may suspect your child is developing an eating disorder and not be sure whether your suspicions are justified. Is she going to the bathroom after a meal? Am I right that he appears to be cutting out certain snacks or eating less at mealtimes? Is she making excuses not to eat, or eat with us? Has he begun to refuse certain foods such as chips, bread, potatoes, butter, meat, or snack foods? Is she eating more snacks and relying on crisps, biscuits, cake, sweets or chocolate – perhaps becoming concerned if your supplies are getting low?

Many parents hope that by leaving the situation alone and not following up those niggling doubts, they will find that the problem is either in their own minds or else will just disappear over time – in other words it will right itself on its own. You may wonder whether talking to your child might actually make matters worse. Maybe your partner, family members, and friends are giving you advice – perhaps conflicting advice – to add to the real dilemma you're facing. You keep turning the advice and the facts over in your mind, but it's so hard to know whom to talk to and what steps to take.

You're not alone

First, let me reassure you that you are not alone and that this stage of suspecting an eating disorder, while very difficult, has been faced by many parents – some of whom you will hear from in this book. You will discover what they did, how they managed, how they felt, what worked for them, and, in some cases, what didn't work – what they wished they hadn't said or tried – which is also useful to know.

I've found that it's really important to discuss your suspicions with someone who has a personal understanding of eating disorders, such as one of ABC's helpline staff,[2] even if they end up not amounting to anything. If they don't, then that's a great relief, but it's important to get information and an informed opinion now, as well as some reassurance and some direction. I know from personal experience that it is wise to seek advice at the earliest stage of concern, to talk it over and "sound it out" with someone who has been where you are now and I once was: worried, suspicious, and not knowing what to do next.

- -

DID YOU KNOW?
FACTS ABOUT WEIGHT LOSS

- *It is possible for children to develop an eating disorder that crosses the boundaries of the separate diagnostic criteria (see Appendix 2) and therefore contains some or even many of the features of other eating disorders. Bulimia does not usually involve weight loss. If your child is losing weight and is also making themselves sick, the illness is more likely to be anorexia with purging.*

- *No child should be losing weight (unless this is medically instigated for health reasons and supervised by a doctor). Anorexia requires vigilance on your part to closely monitor your child's weight loss, particularly in a young child who is growing rapidly. You need to find out their current weight, how much weight they have lost, and what weight they should be for their age and height. You will also need to try to stabilize their weight and monitor any further weight loss quite frequently with the help of your doctor.*

- *Girls' periods stopping can be an indicator of their being underweight. Hormones are fat-soluble and therefore an adequate amount of essential fats is necessary in the diet for hormone production. Periods can start again once fats are reintroduced and a healthy weight is achieved.[3]*

- -

? I've noticed that most of my daughter's lunch is coming back in the lunchbox untouched and that she is trying to avoid food and mealtimes. How should I approach this? Should I be concerned?

If your child's relationship with food or behaviour around food is starting to change, you will have noticed. Avoiding food and avoiding eating at home, when out with friends, or at a café or restaurant are tell-tale signs of a possible eating disorder. It's hard to know if your child is eating their school lunch, so do talk to one of their teachers, asking them to keep it confidential and to be discreetly watchful of your child. Although it might appear difficult for teachers to monitor your child during lunch, or even to check whether they are going in to eat at all, you may have to insist on the grounds that your child's case is a special one, just as those with food allergies would be. We know that many schools are glad to be alerted to a possible problem with food and are vigilant, providing a very useful contact for information and support for you and for your child. Skipping lunch at school, cutting out snacks, refusing certain foods or food groups, reducing portion sizes, or *suddenly* becoming vegetarian or wheat or lactose intolerant are signs that something is not right and needs checking out.

PARENT TO PARENT

We asked her why her packed lunch was returning home some days and she gave good enough reasons. She said she'd been late for lunch so didn't have time to eat it all, or she hadn't liked the lunch I had given her. That was easy for me to change, but it didn't help when I prepared other food for her; she just had other excuses.

She also became sad and rather depressed. She went out on the trampoline all the time and, to begin with, I thought she was just "letting off steam". But I knew in my heart that something wasn't quite right. I tried to comfort her, but I was scared to talk to her about her eating because I didn't know if I'd make it worse. She lacked energy, which I put down to sadness and to the fact that she was only comfortable eating a few items of food, whereas beforehand she had enjoyed food and eaten everything without any problems. Now she'd go into a terrible rage if I tried to get her to eat her normal range of food.

In addition, she wasn't sleeping well and complained of being cold all the time, often wearing baggy clothes and extra jumpers to keep warm (which I later realized also hid her shape and size). She wouldn't talk about eating or what was going on and so I asked her teacher to do some discreet investigating. It was really tempting for me to ask her friends and their families and quiz everybody, but I'd been advised to tell as few people as possible to avoid antagonizing my daughter and making her feel that everybody was talking about her. It was hard enough trying to find out what was going on with her, and I didn't want to drive the problem underground.

Jane

It's important to get as much information as you can to see if there are other people who can help you build up a picture of what's going on. For instance, you may wish to discuss this with your child's mother or father, if they don't live with you, or your child's partner if they are in a relationship. Or perhaps a friend who's had your child for tea or relatives may be able to observe your child's eating habits and report back to you. You will need to be careful, however, not to pressurize or antagonize your child by making them think that you're all talking about them.

PARENT TO PARENT

I asked her dad, who has a new partner, if he'd noticed our daughter being different or unhappy when she was round at his house. Did they have any worries about her and her eating? They were really quite good about it, especially her step-mum who said she'd do some gentle questioning and let me know what she found out. We all wondered whether this was to do with our divorce (and it made me feel really guilty), but we were encouraged that lots of parents are divorced and not all their children have eating problems.

We decided to pull together, all to help her, and not let her do or say one thing in their house and something different at mine. Her step-mum phoned me one day to say that she'd seen her put her packed lunch into the bin at the bus stop on the way to school. Sharing that information helped me confirm my suspicions and helped me realize I needed to talk to my daughter.

Sue

? Our daughter hates her body and says she needs to diet and I'm worried. Could this be the start of an eating disorder?

Unfortunately we live in a very image-conscious time in which how we look is a concern for both boys and girls – as well as for older men and women. Dieting has never been more popular. It is true that many eating disorders do begin with so called "dieting" but usually diets don't last because people don't stick to them and weight quickly goes back on once the diet has ended. At ABC we rarely hear about children who develop an eating disorder by going on a conventional diet. The vast majority turn to restricting their eating owing to unhappiness about themselves and worries about life. Unlike conventional dieting, this can last and can develop into an eating disorder.

Self-hatred extends beyond body hatred and, together with any issues that might have caused it, can often lead to a permanent desire for thinness. When this is the reason for someone dieting, they can be extremely rigid about not eating. Those who can't maintain their control to avoid eating may resort to bingeing and/or purging and, of course, different forms of purging may also accompany weight loss. Although it might be tempting to suggest going to the gym with your child in order to improve their body image, they can think you're telling them they need to lose weight – and by repeatedly going to the gym they may do so. You may be aware of issues contributing to body hatred such as teasing, bullying (including cyber bullying), and abuse which lead to poor self-confidence and low self-esteem.

PARENT TO PARENT

The body hatred upset me greatly because we all saw her as beautiful and had given her nothing but encouragement and praise. We couldn't understand the constant negativity she directed at herself and to parts of her body – constantly looking in the mirror and trying to grab her stomach and saying it was disgusting. We tried arguing with her and persuading her that she was lovely, but it was futile and only made me upset and made me cry.

Our daughter was very bright, a real academic, very determined to be successful at everything. I noticed that her friendships seemed to be changing; I suppose the girls in her year were growing up and some were probably a bit jealous of her academic ability. I thought she was trying to "fit in" more with her peer group – particularly the popular ones – by wanting to look like them and behave like them, but she didn't have a robust temperament and was easily crushed and hurt. We have a good relationship and I knew I needed to get her to talk to me and tell me how she was feeling about her life generally. Fortunately she felt able to share some of her anxieties and her unhappiness, and she said this made her feel much better and supported. I had to pick my moments carefully, though.

Helen

Again, the key thing at this stage is to persevere with trying to talk to your child so that they don't bottle up their feelings. Getting them to open up about the wider issues that are troubling them and encouraging them to be able to trust and confide in you or in someone close to them is vital at this stage. Some people find that their child's negativity about themselves is a phase that passes or that they can actively guide their son or daughter away from developing an eating disorder.

Parent to Parent

It saddened us to find that she had issues of low self-esteem, particularly as we had always shown her our love and felt that we had always affirmed her. We did have some success building her self-esteem and giving her extra praise and encouragement without her thinking we were trying too hard. Yes, her eating – particularly her likes and dislikes of certain foods – were affected for a while, but thankfully she steered herself out of what could have become an obsession. We carried on eating and serving up

21

meals in exactly the same way and I think because we didn't make it an issue, she had scope to eat normally again without losing face.

Sarah

Check Point

Some of the signs that your child may be developing an eating disorder:

- a change in mood – sadness, depression, anger, withdrawal, tearfulness;

- tactics and excuses to avoid eating;

- dieting or refusing certain foods such as fats, carbohydrates, and snacks;

- stress, anxiety, pressure from work or school coupled with a changing attitude towards food or eating;

- friendship and relationship problems in addition to a changing attitude towards food or eating;

- perfectionism and obsession with achievement;

- addiction to sports and exercise, over-exercising;

- complaining of stomach aches and feeling full;

- low self-esteem, body hatred, and self-hatred;

- weight loss unless on a medically instructed or supervised diet.

? **My son has become very sullen and quite obsessed about what he will and won't eat. Should I be worried?**

A change in mood coupled with a growing anxiety about food is often seen at the start of an eating disorder, so, although this could be a passing phase, you would do well to keep a close eye on things. You may notice your child avidly reading the nutritional information on the back of the cereal packet in the morning, for example. They may even mistakenly believe that they need less energy than the calories required by an adult and argue about food and quantities with you. Suddenly refusing food that he has always enjoyed or eaten without any fuss, or starting to dictate to you what he will or won't eat, is a worrying sign.

PARENT TO PARENT

He suddenly began talking about fats and cholesterol and seemed to know the calories of all his food. I thought that it was to do with a healthy eating programme at school to begin with; that he was trying to get as fit as possible. He didn't want to talk to me about anything and his moodiness quickly turned into sullenness and defiance, not helped by the fact that he was eating less.

Everyone told me to "back off" and give him some space, but I thought that that would mean he could do precisely what he wanted and say what he liked. My husband and I weren't prepared to let him do this, so it became a bit of a battle all round really. At the beginning I overreacted and often we came to "blows". Realizing that my husband was better at relating to him and talking to him than I was helped to take a lot of anxiety away from me. My being a little calmer may then have made our

*son less confrontational and it certainly took some
of the pressure off him and the situation.*

*My son's grandma was also a great source of
stability and help. They get on really well and she
can tell him things he'd never accept from us. She
encouraged him to think of his health and, once he
knew how many calories he needed for his health
and development, his knowledge of calories could
be turned to good use, to build him up and make
him feel safe with what he was eating. I don't think
he'd realized how many calories a boy of his age
and height needed, especially when still growing.
I carried on cooking healthily and stressed the
balanced diet and the energy he needed. I think that
knowing how many calories he should actually have
helped him relax a little. It also helped that he really
enjoyed playing football, and we reminded him
that he wouldn't make the team if he became weak.
Football was something that really mattered to him
and motivated him.*

Rachel

? Our daughter complains of stomach aches at mealtimes
and says she can't eat. Could this be an eating disorder?

It is important to distinguish a physical ache from a psychological
one, and to discover whether the physical ache is caused by not
eating enough or by stress and anxiety, or whether there is another
physical cause that the doctor needs to rule out. The need to rule
out a physical reason or illness – for instance appendicitis or IBS –
provides a good reason to get your child to the doctor.

PARENT TO PARENT

The fact that our daughter got stomach ache so often at mealtimes made me suspicious that she might be showing signs of an eating disorder. At first we wondered whether the stomach ache was caused by stress and the fact that our mealtimes were loud and rushed. We therefore tried to eat earlier, or I'd suggest she and I have our dinner in front of the TV, but I also worried that it could be something physical so I made a doctor's appointment for her. The doctor did some checks and a blood test and had a talk to her. Once the results were back, the doctor said there was no physical cause and so we knew that we had to look at the possibility of an eating disorder.

I discovered that our daughter was also making excuses for not eating with us. She would say that either she had just eaten at a friend's house on the way home from college, or that she'd had a big lunch and didn't want what we were having because she was too full and that she'd get something later. I then started to check and realized that she didn't actually have that food later.

I couldn't relax or stop worrying and I started to panic. It really took over my every waking thought, until I was sick with worry each and every day. I couldn't sleep either. I lay awake for hours worrying and going through all the possibilities. The thought of an eating disorder left me completely distraught because I just didn't know how to deal with it. I'd read about it in magazines but, actually, the accounts there weren't very encouraging and all I could remember was the threat of heart damage and possible infertility, the risk of osteoporosis, and other development problems. It's really hard not to dwell on these and fear the worst. I did try to calm myself down and think about the facts before me.

When I sat down and thought about it, I realized that my daughter didn't have time for breakfast, I didn't know what she was having for lunch, and because she often managed to get out of dinner, she must have been eating very little.

Karen

Check Point

Some further signs that your child may be developing an eating disorder:

- lethargy, tiredness, but not sleeping well at night;

- constantly feeling cold, and trying to keep warm with baths/showers;

- wearing clothes that are too big or having to buy clothes a size or two smaller than normal;

- hair loss or hair lacking lustre, growth of fine body hair particularly on backbone or arms;

- periods stopping or failing to start at puberty;

- frequently visiting the bathroom directly after meals;

- signs of vomiting, including raw knuckles, sore throats, or swollen salivary glands.

? We think our daughter is being sick after her evening meal. What should we do?

Making oneself sick (a way of purging) is one very common method for those who want to get rid of the calories they have eaten or the feeling of food in their stomachs. However, those struggling with disordered eating don't realize that purging is not an effective method of weight loss and that it creates far more problems than it solves: a vicious circle, misery, and potential physical problems. One of the first things to do is to find out whether this is happening regularly, and that means listening out and watching for tell-tale signs such as marks around the sink or lavatory or even a freshly cleaned bathroom.

PARENT TO PARENT

It took us a while to suspect that she was making herself sick but we realized that she always went to the bathroom straight after dinner because we continuously heard the loo flush. My wife said that she had noticed that there was always lavatory paper in the loo and that it had always been cleaned (she could smell fresh cleaner and lots of air spray in there).

We weren't really suspicious at first, but then my wife recalled seeing some strange marks in the sink that she'd thought nothing of at the time. Now we started to put things together.

Our daughter had talked about feeling full and bloated but we thought maybe she'd had a snack before dinner on the way home from work. It was her first job and she was finding it quite a strain. She often appeared quite tearful and shattered at the end of the day. My wife noticed that my daughter was buying in extra food that we hadn't asked her to and that some food from the cupboards was going missing. I felt we were spying on her, but we decided my wife would go up and listen near the bathroom door.

The truth dawned on me rather slowly because to be honest I didn't want to consider that my daughter might have a problem with food. I found the thought of her having bulimia quite disgusting, actually: something I couldn't talk about, something other people get – those you read about in the newspaper, but no one I'd know.

But I was faced with the grim possibility that my daughter had bulimia. I thought we'd done something wrong to make her do this. I'll also admit that I couldn't talk about it to anyone else and get help. I saw this as a private matter, something secret and shameful and altogether not normal.

Later of course I realized that actually I was thinking about myself and keeping up appearances. I hadn't considered how my daughter must be feeling having to do this, and actually it nearly broke my heart when I saw it from her perspective, how the stress and strain of her new job were affecting her health and her views about herself.

I believed that she wouldn't want to talk to me, that I should leave all this to my wife to sort out. To be honest, I was out of my depth.

But my daughter **did** need my involvement and my care as well, even though I got it wrong quite often. I had to realize that, looking back at the mistakes I made: the slow start, my failings and my shame, and my dwelling on them just held me back. It struck me that actually the past was past and there *was nothing I could do about it. But what I **could** control, and what would make a difference, was how we all went forward.*

Phil

ACTION PLAN

Suspecting your child may have an eating disorder

- If you think there's something wrong, there probably is, so trust your instincts.

- Try to piece things together. Try not to panic but get as much information as you can in order to build up an understanding of the situation.

- Seek information discreetly from a few significant people such as your child's teacher, best friend, boyfriend, girlfriend, or partner, but avoid alerting lots of people and betraying your child's confidence.

- Ask yourself whether you are the right person to talk to your child. Do you have a strong enough relationship with them at this time, or would they relate better with their father or mother, partner, granny, godmother, or older sibling? If you feel that you are the right person, then listen and chat with them, choosing your time, place and method carefully.

- Try not to concentrate your questions totally on food and eating but more about how they're feeling and coping with life.

- Don't accuse or confront, as it will make your child even more secretive and afraid of sharing with you.

- Try not to let fear make you ignore the situation and don't let yourself be reassured by excuses or other tactics.

- If mealtimes are becoming fraught, try to calm things down and take some pressure off all those at the table.

- Plan to see your doctor alone or with your partner to discuss your suspicions and to learn the approach your doctor would take.

- Consider your own attitude towards food and exercise. If you're dieting or talking about it, are you inadvertently giving your child the wrong messages?

- Don't ignore weight loss, particularly in a child, because they should be gaining weight as they grow. Weight loss needs investigating by a doctor.

CHAPTER 2

Discovering Your Child Has an Eating Disorder

Discovering that your child has an eating disorder is a very shocking and frightening experience. It may be that now, after weeks or even months of suspicion, you're pretty convinced that your fears are founded. On the other hand, you may have discovered that your child has an eating disorder quite suddenly and totally unexpectedly. Maybe you've accidentally come across a diary entry, for example, that really confirms it. Perhaps your son or daughter has confided in you and you now know for certain that they have an eating disorder.

Someone else may even have alerted you: schoolteachers, a colleague of your child, or one of their friends or partner. Or maybe you have arrived at this point just as I did – because you have noticed changes in them, not just in their eating and weight, but also in their mood and personality. I had been aware of signs and symptoms in one of my daughters for a while and suddenly there were just too many to ignore. You may be hoping that if you play it calm, watching without intervening, things may change and your son or daughter may soon be diverted from the brink of an eating disorder and all will be well again. For me this stage didn't last long before I had to come to terms with the fact that my child needed more help than I felt equipped to give, and that something had to be done.

A frightening place to be

I know that where you are now may seem extremely frightening, making you fear the worst and panic – quite understandably. You may have found evidence of behaviours that horrify or even appal you and you can hardly bear to believe it. You may try to deny what you have discovered.

As parents, it is also so common for us to look to ourselves first and even to blame ourselves. Some parents are driven to blame their child or other children and family members for a while – or even each other. Then of course there's the terrifying prospect of the possible damage the eating disorder might inflict on your child's health, the thought of their life being overtaken by the illness or lost to it. All the things you've heard about eating disorders come flooding in and overwhelm you. Or perhaps you know very little about this topic and feel totally out of your depth. I can reassure you that all of these feelings and reactions are perfectly usual and most parents in your situation experience these thoughts on discovering their child's eating disorder. You may also be experiencing denial or even blame from those you expected to listen to you and support you. Now, hardest of all, you have to decide what to do next.

I wonder if, as I did, you can identify with a range of emotions that include not only anguish and deep unhappiness, but also fear, anxiety, despair, anger, and even guilt. Please know you are not alone. We can be very quick to blame ourselves for not having spotted the signs sooner in our children or for not having prevented an eating disorder from developing, but I would urge you not to be harsh with yourself. The important thing now is to concentrate on the positive things you can do to help your child to get through this and to recover from it. Please remember that it is possible to recover fully from an eating disorder, even though the journey can be hard and long.

- -

DID YOU KNOW?
FACTS ABOUT EATING DISORDERS

- *There are three main categories of eating disorders at present: anorexia nervosa, bulimia nervosa, and EDNOS (Eating Disorders Not Otherwise Specified – for more information, see the Diagnostic Criteria in Appendix 2). Binge-eating disorder falls within the EDNOS category. Eating disorders can often seem to start with body hatred and an overwhelming need to be thinner. With bulimia, the sufferer's control over eating breaks down and purging (emptying oneself of food) is thought to provide the weight loss. However, eating disorders can also begin as anxiety or emotional disorders triggered by bereavement, bullying, illness, divorce and separation, redundancy, depression, or abuse. Low self-esteem as well as low self-confidence can often be found at the root of an eating disorder. Styles and patterns of thinking such as perfectionism, black and white thinking, and extremely negative thinking can also contribute.*

- *There is a genetic predisposition towards an eating disorder. This is because personality traits can be inherited and we know that certain personality traits can predispose someone to having an eating disorder. Please note, however, that there is not an anorexic or bulimic gene. You may find that an aunt, uncle or grandparent has had an eating disorder, for instance.*

This knowledge might also alert you to the possibility of a sibling developing an eating disorder.

- *Purging can include compulsive exercise, self-induced vomiting, and abuse of laxatives, diet pills, or diuretics.*

- *A child is still growing until around the age of sixteen, and until then should be gaining weight. Therefore they should not lose weight unless on a medically supervised diet. Extreme weight loss can be life threatening.*

- -

? **Our daughter has told us she has bulimia. We're so shocked and upset and we don't know how to talk to her and how to approach this.**

Those with bulimia are usually very embarrassed, guilt-ridden, and caught in a terrible "restrict–binge–purge cycle" that causes them considerable anguish as well as making them fear that they can never get out of it. Reassuring your child that it is possible to recover, getting them to talk about it and to seek your help is a good start. You will probably be tempted to try to stop them being sick, but by doing this and concentrating on this alone, you can either make matters worse or drive your child into other methods of weight control. Please remember that people often talk of bulimia when in fact their condition is a purging form of anorexia and if this is the case you will have to monitor any weight loss very carefully.

PARENT TO PARENT

To be honest, all I wanted was for her to stop being sick because then I thought everything would be back to normal. I was so upset thinking of her doing this, not just because it's antisocial, but also because she must have felt so awful doing it. It was a terrible shock and worry. I think she was brave to tell us: she must have dreaded seeing us so upset and fearful of what we'd say, how we'd react. It must have been so lonely for her keeping this hidden for so long and living with such a secret. I think that conveying our sympathy and understanding to her (once we'd got over our initial shock) was probably one of the best things to have done.

Next we told her that we didn't know much about this illness, but that we'd get some help together. Fortunately she was at a stage where she was prepared to listen to how we might manage that. I think she knew deep down that bulimia was starting to control her. She told us that it began as a way for her to face her difficulties and to cope better. Now she felt it had total control of her and this frightened her. We found it very hard to understand that she didn't want to keep food inside her and that she saw herself as fat. We also realized that she was losing weight and so we were very worried that this might escalate. Our fears were realized, but she couldn't see the pale gaunt face and frail little body that we saw.

As we got more information we were able to explain to her that this was an illness, one that had got a grip on her, and that it took away opportunities and dreams, as well as physical health. We noticed that not eating and going to the bathroom were worse when she was upset or very anxious, so we tried to help her stay calm and we, as her parents, tried to help her work through her worries and pace her workload

Of course, we both wanted her to see our doctor and she was very reluctant. We talked about *whether she'd prefer to see someone else and she said she'd like to see a female doctor. She asked me if I'd go with her; maybe even go in with her if she felt nervous on the day. I naturally agreed but I thought it best that she write down first what she was going to say to the doctor so she wouldn't be tongue-tied or leave anything out. A part of her was embarrassed about confiding in the doctor and she was also doubtful of the future, the treatment on offer, and whether there really was a chance she could recover. Our doctor advised us to encourage her to believe in recovery and to tell her that many people fully recover. We also reminded her how much we loved her and told her we would be there to support her, come what may.*

Jane

? I've tried talking to my daughter about her eating disorder but she says there's nothing wrong. How can I discover the full extent of the problem?

When you've discovered your child has an eating disorder, the first approach to take is to try to encourage them to feel comfortable talking about it either to you or to someone else. But very often that's easier said than done! It's common for them to shut you out completely and deny that there's a problem. But if you can help them to open up about their feelings generally and provide plenty of opportunities to talk, it will help them move out of the denial stage. If you concentrate all your enquiries on their eating or their weight they may feel threatened and become hostile. This will encourage them to continue to rely on disordered eating as a solution to their problems.

Although you would normally respect your child's privacy, eating disorders are dangerous and potentially life-threatening, so in these extreme cases, we believe at ABC that it is acceptable for parents to look at their child's diary if they happen to come across it – it may well have been left out for parents to find as a cry for help. You may also find it helpful to check their internet history to see whether they have used pro-anorexia or pro-bulimia websites.

PARENT TO PARENT

I found out that this was definitely anorexia one day by complete chance. I was putting some clean washing in her drawer when I saw her open diary. Normally I'd respect her privacy but this was different: I was desperate and felt it justifiable. The diary completely floored me: the anorexia and purging, also the fact that she'd been lying to us all this time, which was devastating. And the way she felt about herself, the impossible weight targets she'd set herself, and the appalling pro-anorexia websites – so-called "Thinspiration" – were unbelievably shocking and upsetting.

I decided to find a good time and to stay calm when talking to her. This was very hard because I just wanted to cry and scream at her that there was no need to do this to herself, that she was lovely just as she was. We did have a fairly calm talk where I reinforced how much we loved her and I asked her what was wrong generally – was she experiencing any problems? – but she refused to open up. She told me that there was nothing wrong and when I said I'd seen her diary she got hysterical, furious with me for "snooping", and said she'd never trust me again, that she hated herself and her life, and that it was all my fault.

I felt pretty shaken but I knew enough to back off and to try another day because I suspected that this was just a knee-jerk reaction, a terrible response to being "found out", and that she would calm down. I decided to wait a while and try again to get her to talk to me. I couldn't sleep so I started composing a letter to her in my mind. I set aside the best part of the next day to write it, carefully choosing the right words and to put what I wanted to say the best way I could.

I put the letter under her door, but she didn't pick it up. It was very distressing but I decided to leave it there and not mention it. The following day I put it on her dressing table and to my dismay when I next went into her room, I found it scrunched up in her bin. I was beside myself with utter desperation. Although I wanted to, I knew I shouldn't confront her but instead wait a while. After a day or so I decided to email it to her to see if that would "reach" her. She did reply to my email as I suppose she didn't have to face me. I can't say that she opened up but she did tell me she'd read my original letter and later I realized that much of it had actually "gone in" and this helped her to turn to us eventually.

Melanie

❓ My son is losing weight. What should I do?

If a child has been a normal weight for their age and height up to now, and has had no medical reasons for weight loss, then they should not be losing weight – any weight – so you should consult your doctor immediately. If you are noticing continual, sustained weight loss – especially if your child is still growing (up until 16 years of age) – then you should consult the doctor urgently and maintain regular contact with them. If your child is an adult who is losing weight unnecessarily then this should also be investigated by a doctor.

PARENT TO PARENT

He was drinking more: water and Diet Coke. I now know that he wanted the drinks to fill him up without taking in any calories. He'd also made excuses to leave the meal table, such as someone ringing him at a certain time about homework, or saying he had a stomach ache and needed the bathroom.

He was also not himself. He was short-tempered and very angry on occasions, emotional and tired all the time. We put it down to his age and his hormones to begin with, but then a few people started to comment on how he was becoming a tall thin streak and my sister asked me if I thought he was losing weight. I felt bad because I hadn't noticed. Perhaps it's harder to see when someone's with you every day and, because my sister hadn't seen him for a while, she'd seen the change in him.

It was good to be able to talk it over with her because she's one of my best friends and she asked me some good questions that got me thinking. What was his eating like? Did I know how much he weighed? Did I know how much weight he'd lost? What weight should he be for his age and height? Was he unhappy? Being bullied? Things like that. I didn't know the answer to many of them and together we decided to do some finding out, without alarming him. Once I knew what I was looking for, it was a bit easier, but still awful. I noticed that he'd play with his food and I found food on the underside of the plate when I took it for washing up. There were even bits of food under the table.

I decided to serve up only his really favourite meals and see if he was off those. I began to watch him when he had his friends round to see if he was having crisps and things with them and to see whether he was eating normally, having no problem snacking. I also wanted to know if he was just filling up before meals as well.

Once I knew that he was deliberately avoiding food I knew I had to find out his weight and see whether he had lost any weight. I contacted the school nurse to see if she had a record of his weight, because my niece's school weighs their pupils each term. Sadly my son's school didn't. The nurse suggested having him go to our surgery nurse to get his weight on the pretext of his tiredness or his asthma check that was now due. In the meantime, we were advised to find out how many calories he needed each day for his age and to be firm with food, trying harder not to let him get away with not eating. This was difficult, but the alternative was to let him carry on losing weight, which we couldn't do.

Sue

Check Point

Some of the signs of an active eating disorder:

- often using the scales;

- food disappearing from your cupboards or larder;

- food being hidden or stored in their rooms, under the bed, in drawers, wardrobe, bags, or anywhere secret;

- finding your child using the bathroom at odd times and directly after meals.

? **We've found bags of old food and sick hidden in his room and don't know how to react.**

This is often how parents know that something serious is happening – and of course it's a terrible shock. Some parents even tell me that mice have got in, or even rats, owing to food being stored. Why do children with some eating disorders hide their sick in bags? Often it's because they are scared to use the bathroom in case they are found out and so they use a bag or something else handy and then find they can't dispose of it. Children often take and store food for bingeing and then can't or don't use it all but wish to keep it for another time. If they suffer from anorexia they may take food with the desire to eat it later and then find they can't but want to keep it nearby. Then they are too frightened to risk being caught trying to remove it.

PARENT TO PARENT

It was such a shock – disgusting too – as some bags of food had been there for weeks, rotting away in his wardrobe. There were also some that contained what looked like old sick. To be honest I didn't know what to think or what to do. Should I just close the door on it and not speak about it? I thought if I did that perhaps he'd clear it himself sometime. I also wondered if he'd left it there for me to find for some bizarre reason.

I also went through all the possibilities: firstly that he had a physical illness he wouldn't talk about or didn't know he had. It occurred to me that we should get him down to the doctor as soon as possible. I then realized that this could perhaps be an eating problem caused by his grandad dying earlier in the year: they had been very close. Our son took it really hard, became very quiet, and went off his food, which was understandable for a while. But then he told us he didn't want to eat meat any more as it made him feel nauseous. We also noticed that he struggled to finish a meal and took forever over it, so that in the end we cleared away.

Looking back, I realized that he'd managed to avoid eating a lot of his meal. It was starting to dawn on me that he was being determined to avoid food and being quite devious. When I thought back I realized that he'd also taken quite a few of his meals upstairs with him. It never occurred to me that he'd hide them and not eat them.

I felt so guilty that I hadn't noticed sooner and that perhaps I should have given him more attention after his grandad had died. I blamed myself for failing to support him. I was completely lost as to what to do. I couldn't tell my friends because it was all so horrible and obviously not normal, and I thought they wouldn't understand or even that they would judge us and change their opinion of our son. I became fiercely protective of him. In fact, he probably knew something was up because I went overboard with enquiries and affection. Then, because I'd bottled up my fears and anguish, I suppose it all came out one day – not the way I'd planned, but it was good to get it off my chest – and actually he seemed a bit relieved that I knew.

His father found the whole thing too difficult to understand to begin with and told him off for upsetting me. "Can't you see what this is doing to your mother and your sister" didn't help our son; it just made him more upset and nervous. In fact it made him eat less, but I could see that his dad was only offloading some of his own fear and that we needed to decide together how we were going to talk properly to our son and help him.

Amanda

Check Point

Some further signs of an active eating disorder:

- seeing bits of food or sick in the sink and around the lavatory;

- a compulsion for strenuous exercise and using exercise DVDs;

- drinking a lot more at the expense of eating;

- chewing gum a lot to "fill them up" or to hide "sicky" breath;

- cutting up meals into tiny portions or pushing food around or under the plate;

- taking forever at mealtimes and storing food up the sleeve or in the cheeks;

- tooth problems, particularly enamel being eroded over a period of time due to self-induced vomiting.

? Why can't she admit there's something wrong?

Eating disorders are coping strategies – a method of dealing with other feelings or events. Sufferers often report that because they are able to exert control over at least some part of their lives – taking in food, or getting rid of it – that this somehow eventually provides an answer to the overwhelming pressures they face in other areas.

Some sufferers find that they do not restrict eating through choice, but that initially they are unable to eat owing to anxiety and feelings that overwhelm them. They may also be driven to repeatedly overeating and eating chaotically because of their emotions. These emotional responses become coping strategies which develop into serious psychiatric illnesses affecting the body and the mind simultaneously. However, the person suffering has become loath to give up their strategy because of fear: fear that without it life would be worse, and fear that there is no hope of recovery. If they haven't begun to contemplate change, then they will be very resistant to it. Those with anorexia really can't see themselves as we do, but often view their reflection in the mirror as fat, ugly, and unacceptable. It's quite usual, therefore, for them not to admit something is wrong, either because they are too scared to do so or because they simply don't believe it themselves. The 1950s study that demonstrates this still provides a sound basis for understanding eating disorders and is still available for you to read.[4]

PARENT TO PARENT

We discovered the eating disorder slowly because she's an adult and no longer lives at home. It was her appearance really. She looked so tired, thin, and drawn. She had obviously lost weight. Once we got over the terrible initial shock we tried to enquire calmly and find out what was wrong with her, but she always brushed our questions away, saying we were concerned about nothing, being overprotective and interfering. We felt completely helpless and of course wished we could have done something sooner. I'd always been very conscious about what I ate and loved exercise so I worried that I'd given her the wrong messages. I had had an eating disorder myself when I was in my early twenties and I now know that my children were likely to be more at risk because of a genetic predisposition.

We found it so hard getting any information because she's an adult, and if she refused to tell us anything, then we felt powerless to make her. So it took a long, agonizing wait. We carried on watching, waiting, and letting her know that we realized she was struggling with eating and that we cared for her deeply. We knew that we couldn't force her to do anything about the eating disorder until she felt ready. We'd remind her of her life ambitions and keep on affirming her, reinforcing her self-worth. We also encouraged her so that hopefully one day she'd turn to us, or someone, admit the problem, and take some steps to get help.

She said that to begin with she really couldn't see what we saw, which we found hard to understand. She couldn't see the sad and emaciated person before us, who'd lost her sparkle and her confidence – someone who'd also become very volatile and aggressive, who'd fly off the handle so easily and who wasn't the daughter we knew and loved and wanted back. Of course, we now realize that she really couldn't view herself the way we did or see what anorexia was doing to her mind as well as her body.

She wanted to hold on to it as it helped her feel better about life. We were shocked to learn that she and others with anorexia really can see themselves in the mirror as huge and hideous. To begin with we wanted to force her to get treatment and we tried to make appointments for her to see specialists, but it only made her avoid talking to us or coming back home and she refused to seek professional help.

It was her boyfriend who handled the situation far better than we did, and he had more influence in reality. He was the one who guided her by getting her to think a bit longer term, about her future, and the future he wanted to share with her. That was the breakthrough.

Anne

ACTION PLAN

Discovering your child has an eating disorder

- Admit the problem to yourself and get help and advice.

- Encourage them to talk to you or somebody else they trust about their difficulties.

- Try to get them to communicate and listen to them without interrupting, avoiding confrontation and arguments.

- Do everything you can to stop them getting anxious, particularly around food or at mealtimes.

- Continue to provide normal meals for them and insist as firmly as you can that they eat these, without coming to blows.

- Tell them that one of the consequences of not eating in terms of lacking energy means that you cannot let them continue doing sport, things at school, hobbies or even going to school, that could cause further weight loss.

- Talk to other members of your family and ask them to avoid continuously probing your child.

- Show unconditional love, support, and understanding despite their behaviour and irrational tendencies.

- Build trust by keeping their confidence.

- If your child is still at school or college have a word in confidence with their tutor or head of year and let them know what is happening. If your child is a boarder then it is very important to keep in regular touch with the school. Ask them to minimize work pressure on your child, observe them generally, and keep a discreet watch at lunchtimes and to report back to you.

- Don't rile or provoke them into further arguments, as this will put up barriers and halt communication.

- Try not to criticize, give orders, or try to "fix" them.

- Don't comment on their appearance or mindset, for example, "You look like a stick insect" or "You're mad".

- Don't blackmail them, for example saying things such as, "Look how you've upset your sister/spoilt family life", and so on.

- Do lean on other members of your family and friends for support, but be prepared for some not being sympathetic.

- Get more information and support for yourselves as parents.

- Encourage them to get help from a doctor, or take them and reassure them about going.

CHAPTER 3

Getting Professional Help

Now that you've discovered that your son or daughter has an eating disorder, you will probably be desperate to find professional help for them and to get some guidance and some support for yourselves. It is very important to seek professional help early, as research shows that the sooner help is found and treatment begun, the better and swifter the recovery.[5]

Your first thoughts are probably about seeking a solution and eradicating the disorder, or about looking to find expert medical advice on stopping the eating disorder from becoming more serious. Although it can still be tempting for some to wonder if engaging professional help will result in reinforcing the disorder so that there's no going back, it really is vital to proceed. Your child needs you to stand with them against the eating disorder and they will probably be too weak mentally – if not also physically – to do this for themselves.

An eating disorder makes people do and say things that are out of character. Eating disorders are complex and contradictory. To those who have little knowledge of them they seem illogical and senseless. The answer seems obvious – to eat more or to stop bingeing, or stop making oneself sick or stop energy-draining exercise, or taking laxatives – but to the person caught in the grip of the illness, the eating disorder is actually a method of coping with life and all its issues. Because the eating disorder is based on short-term thinking, it means that the child you love will go to any lengths in order to retain their eating disorder, believing that that is the solution – the only way of coping with their difficult thoughts and feelings and of feeling in control again. Their minds have also become altered by the lack of nutrition and by any dehydration, and they really are unable to see the danger that they're in and can't simply "snap out of it". Hence they will avoid professional help and treatment. If your child is under sixteen years old, then you have parental authority to seek help for them; after that it is more difficult, but not impossible, to guide them towards it.

First things first

Your family doctor will be your first port of call. An eating disorder can cause serious physical problems and therefore your doctor needs to assess and monitor your child's health. The main purpose will be for the doctor to assess the problem. If your child is suffering from an eating disorder, the doctor will need to find out how long it has been going on for, and then refer your child on to the Child and Adolescent Mental Health Services (CAMHS) or, if your child is over eighteen, to the Adult Eating Disorder Service if necessary. Alternatively, they may discuss other options with you.

The doctor will probably carry out some simple tests, such as taking blood pressure and conducting blood tests to check electrolyte balance (see Appendix 1) and to rule out other medical conditions such as hyperthyroidism or diabetes. Electrolytes are vital chemicals. The balance of these chemicals in the body is essential for keeping the heart beating regularly, as well as for the normal function of the brain – and of course the balance can be upset by poor nutrition and by dehydration.

There may be some things you expect the doctor to do that may not happen, such as weighing your child or even addressing the subject of an eating disorder at all. This is because the doctor will first want to build up trust and monitor the situation over a short period of time. This might alarm and frustrate you, but it could well be a sensible tactic in order to allow your doctor to get involved. You may find that the doctor invites your child back for another appointment on a different topic entirely in order to keep them monitored without raising suspicion and anxiety. If not, don't be afraid to make further appointments and make sure that their health is checked regularly.

- -

DID YOU KNOW?
FACTS ABOUT GOING TO THE DOCTOR

- *Regular medical monitoring is essential for an eating disorder because these are life-threatening conditions. Your doctor will need to keep blood pressure checked to make sure the patient's heart is sound. They will also need to check weight and ascertain any weight loss and do some blood tests to rule out other physical causes for weight loss.*

- *Please remember that a child under sixteen years old should not be losing weight unless they are medically supervised.*

- *Most sufferers are very afraid of seeing the doctor for a variety of reasons. Some fear the eating disorder being taken away or being ordered into hospital and some even fear mention of an eating disorder on their health record.*

- *Remember also that psychotherapy is an important part of treatment and can be accessed independently if necessary alongside medical monitoring.*

- -

? What's the best way for us to approach the doctor and what will they do?

It's a good idea to think about which doctor in your practice you would feel most comfortable going to, and who you think might understand emotional difficulties. Making a checklist of what you want to say, including the facts that you know, is always a good start, and consider writing the doctor a letter ahead of your visit. Your child may prefer to speak to the nurse to begin with, or to see their university doctor rather than your home doctor, so do think about which medical professional would be best initially and where.

PARENT TO PARENT

Of course I played the whole appointment over and over in my mind before getting into the doctor's. I presumed I would have only ten minutes and I should have thought to ask for a longer appointment when I booked, but I wasn't thinking straight. I was so tired. I knew that this doctor in the practice was pro-active. I chose her to write to beforehand because I wanted her to know the facts we'd discovered, and because I thought I'd be too emotional to talk to the doctor when I was there. I also thought that I might forget to say some important things.

The doctor was really good and she asked me if I thought I could get my daughter to come in. I knew it was important and that she'd be agreeable even if we had to be a bit crafty. The doctor told me what she would and wouldn't do on the first appointment. She said she'd prefer to have a general chat with my daughter and ask her questions about life to see if she could get a rapport, and that she might not weigh her right away. She'd see how my daughter reacted to her, to her questions, and how easily she could put her at her ease.

She also said that she'd ask her if her periods had started and that she'd talk to her about the connection between them and eating well, with sufficient essential fats in her diet. She said she didn't think it wise to tell my daughter all the health implications of the eating disorder as she might "switch off", but that she would talk about a few of them. She asked me about my daughter's interests and hobbies too, so as to motivate her.

We didn't have a problem getting her to come to the doctor with me. I let the doctor speak and the two of them talk. It was hard not chipping in all the time and I did have to on some occasions because my daughter withheld some of the facts that I thought were vital. She didn't like me for that, but that was too bad and fortunately it didn't have too much impact on our relationship once we'd left the doctor.

As to her weight, the doctor said that she could see that my daughter was very slim and asked if she'd noticed other things such as feeling tired, feeling cold, or feeling unhappy. This was quite clever, I thought, because my daughter felt able to talk about these aspects to deflect the doctor from closer examination of her weight. The doctor was then able to do some tests for anaemia and thyroid function and to get her back the following week for an appointment to discuss the results. I felt that she had the situation under control and was delighted that she phoned me in the week to say that once the results were in she'd weigh my daughter and check her height to see how far from the normal she was *for her age. I felt reassured and supported as she knew how to handle this.*

Jane

❓ What help is available?

It's tempting to think that you are completely alone because suddenly you feel you're in uncharted waters. Of course, it's easy to panic and therefore not to think straight. The NHS does have an Eating Disorder Service for adults, as well as for children and adolescents within the CAMHS, and it's very important to use the doctor as your support, as well as your child's support both medically and in terms of making referrals for specialist services. Further support includes counselling, dietary advice, support groups in some parts of the country for sufferer or carer, and advisory organizations, details of which are included at the end of this book.

PARENT TO PARENT

I made an appointment to see my doctor alone to explain what was happening. He told me about support groups for people with eating disorders in our county. There was one for carers which I thought it would be good to attend. I met other parents there who, like us, were coping with their children's disturbed behaviour and eating difficulties. I found it really comforting to know that they were struggling just as we were. Some were further ahead and were coming out the other side, so it gave me hope. Listening into the conversations and eventually sharing something of our situation helped me to think differently about what we were trying to do to help my daughter. It gave us some tips.

My husband wouldn't go – he said it wasn't for him, that it was bad enough having the problem we had within the family without taking on other families' problems, but that was how he viewed it. He doesn't confide in a group situation and I think he was frightened that he might hear stories of gloom or failure. I didn't see it like he did, but we're all different. I gained a lot and shared what I'd learned with him.

My doctor also said that if need be he would refer our daughter to the Eating Disorder Service through the NHS, or if we had some private health cover then we could see a consultant privately for initial assessment and diagnosis. He also said that the surgery could provide a counsellor for us although there would be a short wait, and that he could get the dietician in for us to talk to. I can't tell you what a relief it was to know that there was a team of people we could all turn to – our daughter, my husband, and I.

I thought the doctor would say that he couldn't discuss her with me because she was over eighteen, but he said that I was entitled to come and discuss anything that was concerning me and affecting my health, which of course our daughter's weight loss and sickness were. I was having panic attacks and he thought seeing a counsellor would be good for me too. He talked to me about how we could get her into the surgery to see him, although he warned me that she could refuse. He also told me that he would be unable to discuss her case with me if she came to see him but that he would try to arrange for us to have some family therapy.

Christine

Check Point

Information about getting medical help:

- Regular medical monitoring is essential for someone with an eating disorder.

- Don't believe your child if they say they won't go to the doctor. It could be just fear and, if you take them at their word, you may prevent them from changing their mind and give them the option not to go and for their eating disorder to control you.

- Doctors can "fit you in" at short notice for urgent appointments, and you can ask for a home visit if your child needs to be seen and is being difficult. This is something that nowadays we forget and is so useful. Parents often overlook this kind of intervention, which can also act as an incentive for someone refusing to be seen.

- There can often be a wait for a referral to the CAMHS or to the Adult Eating Disorder Service, so ask your doctor to make a referral early and chase it up if need be.

? My daughter refuses to see the doctor. What can I do?

Those struggling with eating disorders are usually frightened of seeing the doctor because they fear the eating disorder being discussed or taken away from them, and that the doctor might be angry with them or force them into hospital. So they may tell you they won't go when actually they might, so don't take them at their first word. If you give a younger child the choice of whether or not to see the doctor you've given them the control. It is important that your son or daughter receives a medical assessment and regular medical monitoring so do try to guide them towards seeing their doctor.

PARENT TO PARENT

She point-blank refused to go and we felt completely thwarted. I wanted to just march her in there for her to listen to the doctor and start to eat again. I felt my authority was being completely ignored and we got into quite a few arguments over this. In the end, I knew I had to calm it all down. Once we realized how frightened she was of giving up the eating disorder, we were able to talk to her about the need for a health check, just to make sure she didn't become so ill that she needed hospital. She was a bit old for the sort of rewards that a younger child might respond to, but she was looking forward to seeing a new film with us and so we said we'd go to the cinema after the doctor's, which might have helped.

Actually, once she saw we weren't backing down but calmly believing that she'd go with us, she did give in, although she said she wouldn't say a thing when she got there. That was another bit of defiance really, more showing how upset she was – so we accepted it and left it at that. In reality that's not what happened. She did go with us, although she refused to let us come in with her.

She had become unusually defiant for her age and her personality. We didn't recognize our lovely girl and we were at our wits' end with her behaviour and her insistence on not eating. My wife was devastated and needed not only some good support, but also useful suggestions on how to manage mealtimes. She had succeeded in persuading our daughter to see the school counsellor as we knew it was important for her to discuss her feelings, but the counsellor said she didn't have much experience with eating disorders. We also needed to know how much lower in weight she could get before it was dangerous and what we should do to stabilize her weight and help her regain the lost weight. I can't say our doctor supplied the strategies but he did do the medical checks and referred her on to the next stage for treatment. That was a relief.

Richard

Check Point

Further information about getting medical help:

- You can access medical and therapeutic consultation and treatment via private hospitals.

- Some private health insurance policies will cover consultations and even a period of treatment.

- There are various support groups that you can contact (see Useful Contacts section).

- Counsellors with varying degrees of experience in eating disorders are available across the UK. Make sure that the counsellor is fully qualified and accredited (see Useful Contacts section).

- An advocacy service exists to help you if you feel your child's treatment is not adequate.

? Our doctor isn't taking this seriously. What can I do to get him to help us?

Many people have really understanding and supportive doctors. Since eating disorders are a growing concern, you would imagine most surgeries have at least one person who has an interest in eating disorders. All doctors were sent the NICE guidelines for eating disorders in 2004; these guidelines set out best practice for doctors and all other medical professionals. It can be the case that boys are slower to be diagnosed because a lot of exercise is normal for boys, and of course they don't have periods which, when they stop, can be indicative of a problem. However if you find that your doctor is not recognizing the problem you are facing, appears unsupportive, or is slow to refer your child to more specialist services, then you may need to tactfully remind him or her of the duty of care outlined in the NICE guidelines.

PARENT TO PARENT

We had read the NICE guidelines as soon as we suspected a problem, and knew we should expect our doctor to listen to us and to follow up our concerns. We explained that we'd noticed our son madly exercising – going to the gym more and more – and that he'd lost weight, but that he was also withdrawn and depressed.

The doctor made me out to be a fussy mother and said that exercise was normal for boys. He told my son that he understood him trying to get a six-pack, which wasn't what we wanted to hear. I felt that the doctor really wasn't taking our son's weight loss seriously even when I explained how much he was exercising and how he'd cut down on his eating. I can't explain the let-down, the hopelessness I felt when the one person I counted on to help me just dismissed my real concerns and the evidence before him. The doctor told my son that he was probably just going through a growth spurt and we shouldn't worry, but I knew that boys need even more calories than growing girls and I wasn't prepared to be "fobbed off".

I rang to speak to the doctor the next day and he did arrange for my son to see the nurse later in the week for some blood tests. I think the doctor was at least willing to see that there might be a physical reason for his weight loss and was prepared to investigate that by doing some blood tests. So that was a start and actually, as we kept up the relationship with our doctor and I kept on supplying new concerns, not only from us but also from his school, we did find that the doctor was more able to see that this was indeed an eating problem if not an eating disorder.

As he got to know our son and how badly he felt about eating and about himself, the doctor did refer our son for specialist help. I'm still shocked that the doctor didn't take the weight loss seriously, because our son was still growing. He'd never been a skinny boy and although there are many healthy skinny boys, we knew that continuously losing weight is not normal in a child. Of course, in conjunction with all of his other issues, I thought we'd get greater understanding more quickly. We also could have done with more support and guidance in how to stabilize his falling weight and manage his eating and the mealtime horror. Thankfully the doctor did monitor our son's weight and give him a series of appointments for blood tests and blood pressure testing.

Caroline

61

ACTION PLAN

Getting professional help

- If you haven't already done so, go and see your doctor on your own or write them a letter before the appointment to explain the situation you're facing.

- Ask if they might be able to book a longer appointment to give you more time to chat, or suggest that you come in at a quieter time of day.

- If you know your doctor well, then an appointment with them will hopefully make this first visit easier. If you are unsure which doctor to see, then have a think about the doctors you know there and whom you would feel most relaxed talking to.

- You could also chat to the practice nurse or ask the receptionists if any of the doctors have a particular interest in emotional health.

- If you can, accompany your child for their first visit to the doctor and take the facts with you. This is easier if your child is under sixteen or, if they are older, if they would like you to be there.

- Approach the school nurse for help and support.

- Your child can ask someone else (a friend or family member) to help them approach the doctor or the receptionist verbally or in writing.

- Your child could see the doctor about another medical matter and get a feel for their manner and the approach that they'd take.

- If your child is an adult who is refusing treatment, try to explain to them that medical check-ups do not put pressure on them to go ahead with treatment, but they safeguard their health and prevent them from sudden collapse or being somewhere that they never planned to be, such as in hospital or laid off from work.

CHAPTER 4

Managing Your Child's Eating

The sad fact is that once an eating disorder has got a grip, then eating (which formerly presented no problems) now becomes a major issue, and food (once a pleasure or at least satisfying hunger) is now a cause of arguments and a deep concern. Parents expect older children to eat and don't imagine having to persuade them at their age, even though they may have been fussy toddlers or still have some dislikes, as most of us do. So you will have taken eating for granted as I did and as everyone usually does.

Enjoyment, comfort, celebration, and hunger, together with our natural appetite – our mind's and body's need for nutrition – should enable us to eat in a normal manner quite easily and regularly. Sometimes too much, sometimes too little: normal eating means that we trust our body to make up the difference. There isn't deep or prolonged guilt about food or lists of good or bad food – food to be avoided with fear and dread. Life does not consist of thinking about food or planning how to avoid it or get rid of it, unless, of course, the person concerned is suffering with an eating disorder. Sadly, you now have to contend with these thoughts about food and eating. You'll hear them voiced and you will need to try to persuade your child to eat normally or regularly – or even to eat at all.

Pressure at mealtimes?

Perhaps your child is criticizing your eating habits, your cooking, even the size and shape of others, sometimes even with some spite, which may be really out of character for them. Perhaps you are aware that your child is wanting to cook, has become obsessed with recipe books, and is baking for the whole family (as my daughters did), enjoying watching you eat the results but having nothing themselves. Alongside this, eating together has now become associated with fear, unhappiness, guilt, anger, avoidance, refusal, and rejection. Rows occur over food for the first time and mealtimes – whether they are round a table or not – become fraught with difficulties.

If you are the cook or provider, then you will doubtless be anxious about what to serve up and whether or not it will be eaten. At some stage it is very likely that the person with the eating problem will be standing over the cooking process quizzing the cook about the ingredients and demanding to know things like: "How much oil did you put in there?" or "Did you add sugar?" Tantrums and excuses are usual: "You know I can't eat butter, why did you put it in? I can't eat that meal now." I remember how trips to the shops or supermarket become not just a chore but also a hugely stressful and vital task, one that was fraught with many emotions.

Eating disorders cause great anguish to us as parents, and also to siblings and to other family members, especially grandparents, uncles and aunties who find that meals out or meals at their homes are no longer enjoyable or even possible. Family get-togethers or people's birthday celebrations are ruined with tension and tears.

For those of you who are facing bulimia you will probably be seeing food disappearing from your cupboards, as I did, sometimes in vast amounts and with a financial cost. You may be aware of foods being secreted or hidden and there will be arguments about it – if not between you and your child then perhaps between your child and their siblings as *their* sweets go missing, *their* box of chocolates gets taken.

Of course if your child is suffering with anorexia, your chief concern is to prevent further weight loss and somehow to encourage your child to eat foods that they are frightened of and utterly refusing to eat, in the hope that they might stabilize or even put back some of the lost weight. They will be terrified of any weight gain. Knowing what they should eat is not the problem; it's getting them to eat when they are determined not to.

- -

DID YOU KNOW?
FACTS ABOUT FOOD AVOIDANCE

- *Choosing what to eat is agonizing for someone with anorexia, and yet, as parents, we so often give that choice to them, leaving them to decide what they "want". Someone who doesn't want to eat many calories – fats, or carbohydrates – will inevitably choose something very low in energy value.*

- *Be aware of your child eating lots of salad, fruit, and low-calorie foods such as Quorn products, rice cakes, and crisp breads, or filling up with water or fizzy drinks.*

- *Be wise to the deceptive "tricks" used by someone determined to avoid food or mealtimes.*

- *There is an anxiety-based disorder called Food Avoidance Emotional Disorder. This shares the symptoms of anorexia nervosa with the main exception that sufferers with FAED can recognize that they are very slim and need to put on weight, and usually try to do so but cannot.*

- -

? **Mealtimes are fraught with emotion and unhappiness for our daughter, for us and for our other children. Is this normal?**

When trying to manage an eating disorder it is usual for parents and siblings to absolutely dread mealtimes. You feel you're either continually nagging or fretting about how much food or how many calories you can get into your child, while having to "tread on eggshells" around the subject. You are so aware of how dangerous it is for them to be either eating so little day-by-day or bingeing and purging, and so your fears are mounting. You may also be looking at someone each day who has severe emaciation and the agony of your worry and heartache is unbelievably hard to bear. The evening meal can be the worst because there's a build-up of tension over the day as a result of all the failed attempts to get them to eat well or adequately.

PARENT TO PARENT

When it came to preparing and serving something for all the family I was tired out and petrified that as usual she'd refuse the meal or cut up her meagre portion into tiny little bits. I feared that every day that went by like this was another day closer to her being taken into hospital or worse. All my attempts at persuading her – cooking things she liked, and later the things she dictated – took away my control too. She was only eleven years old, but she refused to listen to all reason.

I felt I had no one to support me as I tried to coax her and then did battle. My other children were astounded that she was getting away with such defiance, but they also realized that her behaviour at the table was abnormal. Her outbursts could be shocking and made my younger child cry. I think in the end she started to get on their nerves. Her older sister often yelled at her that she was ruining everything and, although I stood up for her, in my heart I had to agree.

That started a period of her not sitting with us but standing away from the table near the cooker, refusing to sit down and join in with us. This was very difficult to deal with because actually we were all so weary that it was almost preferable to have her away from us. I knew, though, that it would be very hard to get her to eat anything if I allowed her to stand there, so I got my younger daughter to ask her to come back, saying she missed her sitting next to her at the table, which was true, actually. It worked because I think she needed an excuse to back down and I don't think she would have done it for me.

My younger daughter got her to do some drawing with her while they ate. I hadn't allowed this before, but it broke the silence, gave them a focus other than the food, and the atmosphere was better. In the early days I let my other children leave the table if she sat there playing with her food. Later on I was advised to let them encourage her to eat what she had on her plate by suggesting they all went to watch a DVD together or something on TV once she'd finished. That worked quite well sometimes – otherwise we'd be there for hours.

Jane

? How can we stop our daughter from binge eating?

People tend to binge on the things they like and miss. It is a result of their trying to eat so little, failing, and then feeling guilty. Once their control breaks down they tend to binge on high energy, high sugar foods such as cakes, biscuits, bread, chocolate, and cereal, often in vast amounts. Once bingeing has occurred the "restrict–binge–purge cycle" is started again. So, in conjunction with professional psychotherapy, input from the dietician, and medical monitoring, it is important to help your child try to normalize their eating and to eat sufficient, well-balanced meals three times a day, even though this can be very difficult to achieve.

PARENT TO PARENT

To begin with we couldn't believe that she was bingeing because she ate a normal meal with us on the occasions we all sat together. On the other evenings I watched her get herself something quite normal and adequate. I couldn't understand why she stole and smuggled into her room all the foods she said she so despised. She hated herself for having to do this, and would resolve the next day to eat even less. For a few days she might succeed, although she was irritable and often foul-tempered, lashing out at everyone. She was impossible to reason with.

I was utterly horrified to find out what she did eat in secret: huge bowls of cereal, cakes, packets of biscuits, bars of chocolate, and several packets of crisps. She even went through a whole box of chocolates I'd been given for my birthday. I did challenge her on this and, yes, it did end up in a monumental row. I said I couldn't afford to keep restocking the cupboards every few days and that it wasn't fair on her brother who sometimes had his treats "stolen".

Once we'd calmed down I asked her to tell me what made her do this. She admitted that she was trying to diet because she hated herself so much.

I listened and it was really upsetting to hear. She said that she dreamed about food and trying to avoid it made her hungrier, so she found she couldn't control herself and went to the cupboard in secret to "stuff myself and make myself hurt as a punishment for being so weak and so useless".

I asked her what I could do to help and she said she wanted me to help her stay more in control. I replied that I could only do that if she was honest with me and told me when she felt the urge to binge. I said that she needed to have more to eat during the day. That way I thought she'd be less empty and less likely to binge.

The dietician advised us to persuade her to have some slow-release carbohydrates such as porridge in the morning, and brown rice or jacket potatoes in the evening. We were told that she shouldn't try to fill up on sweet stuff as this was addictive and empty energy. I also offered not to do a big weekly shop so that there wouldn't be quite so much to tempt her and she liked that idea. I cut down on the amount of snack items I bought for the family although I didn't banish them. I wanted to let her know that these were OK in moderation – and my son would have protested! I offered to hide some food away or even get a lock for the cupboard, but she said that perhaps we could leave that until absolutely necessary.

She said the evenings were the worst time for her, especially if something had happened during the day to upset her, so we stayed together during the evenings and played computer games or watched some TV together, which helped distract her. It all helped prevent her from bingeing so often while we were waiting for counselling for her.

Gill

Check Point

Some key points to remember when preparing meals:

- The real and intense fear of gaining weight for someone with an eating disorder is far from the usual small dissatisfaction many people might experience.

- Your eating disorder dietician will suggest that you agree a meal plan together, rather like a contract between you, including certain conditions and incentives as well as a range of food across the food groups if possible.

- Giving your child too much choice early on in their eating difficulties quickly gives them authority and control over your cooking and what they will or won't eat.

- Easily accepting that your child dislikes or won't eat certain foods or food groups means they cannot change their minds about it, even if they'd like to.

? How do we help stop our daughter's weight loss?

The longer the weight loss continues, the harder it is to regain the weight because the calories required to restore 1 kg a week (2.2 lb) in a child are 1,000 extra calories a day.[6] On average, a child needs between 1,500 and 2,500 calories a day (depending on their level of activity) in order just to maintain their normal weight. Therefore, to gain 1 kg a week, their daily calorie allowance will need to be increased to between 2,500 and 3,500. A growing child should also be gaining weight irrespective of any height increase every three months in addition to their normal weight for height and age until they are sixteen years old. It is not unusual for a young child to be gaining 5-6 kg a year.

If weight declines, the mind finds it harder to fight against the desire for weight loss. Those with anorexia believe that any little weight gain will make their weight balloon out of control and this fear is exaggerated the lower in weight they become, resulting in terror. Making sure they receive the calorie allowance they need is, of course, much easier said than done, and something that you should seek advice on from your child's doctor, who will refer you to specialist services in order to support your efforts. It's here that the dietician and other staff experienced in eating disorders will help advise you about dietary intake.

PARENT TO PARENT

We managed to restore our daughter's lost weight for almost a year. She always listened to us and was pretty easy-going until anorexia and bulimia made her behave quite differently, but that came later on. It wasn't easy to persuade her to eat, not at all. She did try to resist – arguing, pleading, and crying – but we stood firm and she agreed to draw up a meal plan with me, based on calories. This was something that her psychiatrist at the CAMHS supported too, so we were both reinforcing the same method of weight gain. I know that many people might wonder if knowing calories would make her see every item of food in terms of calories, but actually somehow she knew all about them anyway.

I also know we worried that, once she was on a calorie-counted weight-gaining plan, she might become hooked on counting calories for life. However, after a year at home, then five months at a specialized eating disorders clinic, followed up with months on a calorie-maintenance programme, she did eventually learn to eat freely. Today she eats without any problems whatsoever. Her weight is normal; she never thinks about calories or her actual weight; she enjoys food again and eating with friends and family.

She liked having a calorie-controlled plan because she said it made her feel safe. The consultant set how many she needed each day and it surprised her that the amount was more than the suggested guidelines of 2,000 calories a day for women. The consultant reminded her that she needed more because she was still growing and needed to gain extra weight. As long as she kept all her meals, snacks, and drinks to the quota, then she was prepared to continue.

The first week before she was weighed was obviously the hardest. Once she saw that she'd made the correct increase it was a little easier for her to bear because she'd imagined that she'd put on a stone or more, which we had to keep reminding her just wasn't possible.

I did find it very hard to begin with, but there are several well-known cookery books that give the calories in all the dishes, so all I had to do was follow the recipe instructions completely and calculate the calories in any portion I wanted. This meant weighing the empty dish first and then again with the cooked meal in it. By subtracting the weight of the empty dish I then had the net weight of the meal. The net weight equates to the number of calories stated for the whole dish, so to get the number of calories per gramme I divided the total number of calories by the net weight. Once I had the calories for 1g I could then calculate the number of calories for any weighed out portion. For example, if a whole dish of shepherd's pie has 2,500 calories in it and the net weight is 1,000 g, then divide 2,500 by 1,000 to find out how many calories there are in 1 g. In this case, 1 g has 2.5 calories, so 100 g would therefore have 250 calories and 200 g would be 500 calories. Once I'd done the main dish, I would then work out the extras – potatoes, for instance, or other vegetables – with the help of a calorie-counting book.

It seemed pretty miserable and time-consuming at first, but once I'd done the calculations for one particular meal I wrote it down so that the next time I came to do that meal I could do it easily. Once I had the calories for 1 g of any home-cooked meal it was easy to serve up a portion with the calories required without fuss and with confidence by multiplying the number of grammes to obtain the necessary calories. Of course there were times when I relied on ready meals which had the figures pre-calculated, but I felt that home cooking got her used to normal eating again. We had quite a few arguments with her because she didn't trust me to weigh it properly – she was so frightened I'd exceed the calories – but I reminded her that there would be no point in my doing that – it would just ruin our contract. Anyway, she could see the weight gain of only a steady 1 kg (2.2 lb) per week when she went for her appointment at the CAMHS.

It was important to let her know that if for any reason her weight gain increased by over 1 kg during the week, then we'd drop the calories by 250 one day at a time until she was back to her weekly target weight.

Jane

Check Point

Further key points to remember when preparing meals:

- Animal protein builds muscle and body tissue better than vegetable protein does.

- Extra energy in terms of calories can be added to meals without adding bulk, by using a higher calorie cereal, for instance, or even nuts as well as drinks such as smoothies or milkshakes.

- Although build-up drinks such as Complan are available from supermarkets and chemists, and Fortifresh, Fortisip, Ensure, or Pediasure are available on prescription, they can have fewer calories than a smoothie or milkshake that contains "real" food, fats, and equally good nutrition.

- Be careful not to ignore the needs of your other children when it comes to their food and what they enjoy eating.

- Just because one child may need their diet supplemented, it doesn't mean that everybody needs to eat more. However, as parents you may feel you have to match the diet of your child for the period of their weight restoration in order to encourage them.

❓ He won't eat carbohydrates or fats and watches over me as I cook. What should we do?

Cutting down on carbohydrates or fats and having a "good foods/ bad foods" list in their mind is often one of the first signs that a child's eating has changed for the worse and that they have developed a phobia about certain food groups or items. You will have tried to reassure your child that a range of items from all the food groups are vital for health. Undoubtedly you will have tried to include fats and carbohydrates in their diet, which are all essential, and sometimes you will have had to add fats to the meal you are making without your child noticing. Watching over the cook is another sign of extreme anxiety over the ingredients of a meal and demonstrates a growing phobia about particular foods. Making meals in advance, keeping him out of the kitchen – maybe distracting him with other occupations – and enlisting the help of others are all things to try.

PARENT TO PARENT

He tried to avoid pasta and cereals altogether, saying that these carbohydrates gave him indigestion and made him feel bloated. We wondered whether he had a wheat intolerance. Taking him to the doctor didn't rule this out straight away, so I allowed him to exclude these, although I did continue to serve potatoes as he was very fond of jacket potatoes. Maybe because he was still relatively young and fairly naive, he didn't think that potato was a carbohydrate, but for whatever reason he accepted them in his diet, although chips, of course, were out of the question, as were all other foods with added fats.

To begin with, I traded on this naivety and cooked before he came home from school. I would add some butter into the mashed potato as normal; he didn't notice this as I'd always added it in. I also added some cream to the custard although I was petrified that he'd taste it and stop eating it. I found that if I spread butter on the bread for his sandwiches and kept spreading then I could get more in and it almost disappeared. It might seem sad, but I was desperate to get some extra calories in and a range of nutrients without him noticing.

Gradually he became more panic-stricken about food. It became a real phobia for him, whereas in the past he'd eaten anything and everything, just like his sister. It was so awful to see him worrying about every item of food on his plate. His anxiousness made him ask hundreds of questions about his meals. He wanted to know how I cooked them and what ingredients I used.

It was really stressful, and hard not to get annoyed having him watch over me when I cooked. He said he wanted to become a chef and asked for cookery classes, but we were advised that this was likely to be the result of his eating disorder so that he'd probably change his mind, but that we could use it as an incentive for when he was back to a healthy weight. We did ask his rugby coach to talk to him about healthy eating as our son admired him.

I carried on making the meal in advance whenever I could. His consultant said that he was not to be in the kitchen when I was preparing food; that he had to learn to trust me. I hadn't thought of removing him from the kitchen but it did help a lot. He didn't like being out of the kitchen before meals but we carried on insisting and when he argued we told him we were carrying out the consultant's wishes.

Julie

ACTION PLAN

Managing your child's eating

- Find out how much your child weighs now, either from the scales at home or at the doctor's, consultant's, or school nurse's.

- Find out what weight your child should be for their age and height from ABC, from your doctor, or from the Child Growth Foundation.[7]

- Work out how many calories they are actually consuming each day and how many they need. It will usually be at least 2,000 a day – more when growing, very active, or needing to gain weight.

- Set a target and find ways of slowly working towards that target weight, gaining 1 kg (2.2 lb) per week at a time. This is a small but manageable amount for a sufferer.

- Try to agree a meal plan together – a contract or deal between you – including certain conditions and incentives as well as a range of food, across the food groups if possible.

- Consider asking the school to allow you to share a packed lunch with your child outside school, perhaps in the car or in a café, or to let them come home to you for lunch if convenient.

- Use a calorie-counting book to weigh the portions of food items to be served.

- Consult a dietician via your doctor or privately and work with the Eating Disorder Service asking for their advice and a joint approach.

- Keep an eye on your child's weight weekly by weighing them at home or at the doctor's/consultant's.

- Keep the scales under your control.

- Try to keep mealtimes as normal as possible (although this is so hard to do) and be consistent in your approach as parents.

- Sit alongside your child while they eat and encourage them, setting a time limit or being there however long it takes.

CHAPTER 5

Managing Your Child's Emotions

Eating disorders are complex psychiatric conditions that simultaneously affect the mind and the body. The way the sufferer thinks about themselves and begins to unravel their relationship with food, finally finding some relief from the relentless mental anguish of the eating disorder, is usually addressed during counselling using psychotherapy, which forms a very important part of treatment. The emotional aspect of an eating disorder also means that parents, siblings, and partners have to face and cope with a troubled mind, day in, day out. You will find your role has suddenly become "untrained psychiatric nurse, on call 24/7."

Unless you have had an eating disorder yourself or have supported someone through one, the emotional side of it will be a huge shock to you. You could be quite unaware that eating disorders affect the mind of the sufferer and that this causes unbelievable stress, tension, and misery to them and to those who love them.

Eating disorders are rarely about weight, size, or image. The fact is that we do not yet fully understand why some people are more disposed than others to use food as a coping method for life. Sufferers are people who may not have developed good coping strategies and sufficient resources. They may have certain thinking styles that make them more susceptible to an eating disorder. Some people find that their eating disorder begins as an emotional response or disorder – an anxiety problem, for instance. Their emotions cause them to lose the ability to eat or, contrarily can lead them to eat too much. Sometimes eating disorders are part of another mental illness.

What triggers an eating disorder?

Eating disorders are very complex and there isn't a single cause. There are genetic, biological, cultural, and psychological factors underlying an eating disorder, some or all of which contribute to its development. There are also many factors that can trigger an eating disorder, for instance bullying, stress, bereavement, family breakdown, and even domestic and sexual violence. Unfortunately many people are unaware that there are these causes, concentrating their view – sometimes a dim view at that – on the outward physical consequences of the eating disorder, notably weight loss and physical side effects. Apart from showing little understanding of what might have triggered this response in someone, such a view also ignores the relentless agony for sufferers and loved ones alike.

For those with bulimia, who usually remain at a normal weight, and those with binge-eating disorder, who are overweight, their mental anguish, the self-loathing, the guilt, the secrecy, shame, and loneliness, together with the constant thinking and worrying about eating may remain hidden. This leaves sufferers and their families feeling not only alone but also misunderstood and even judged.

As parents, you will doubtless recognize – even if you do not fully understand – the mindset of an eating disorder: the negative self-criticism your child voices; their obsession about weight; the overwhelming fear of weight gain; panic about food at home and particularly when out; the moods and aggressive speech; accusations, swearing, and rages, which can even result in physical violence against you or directed at themselves. You will also probably experience their hopelessness, timidity, fear, clinginess, misery, and depression. "My daughter behaves like a ten-year-old little girl again and although she's a grown-up I am back to protecting her and caring for her as I did all those years ago," said one mum. "Worse still, I don't know how to help her change the way she thinks of herself and I don't know if we'll ever get our lives back."

So many deep and troubled thoughts and feelings coexist for the sufferer that your role of encouraging your child and combating their constant negativity and anguish can be a monumental task.

- -

DID YOU KNOW?
SOME FACTS ABOUT ANXIETY SURROUNDING EATING DISORDERS

- *Anorexia nervosa was first used as a term in 1873, although cases of those with an apparent loss of appetite were recorded in the seventeenth century.*

- *Bulimia nervosa was first used as a term in 1979, although cases were documented hundreds of years ago.*

- *The word "nervosa" shows that both anorexia and bulimia are anxiety related.*

- -

? Our daughter has extreme emotions; she cries, gets angry, and easily falls into rages. Is this normal and how can we help her and our family cope?

More often than not, parents have never heard their son or daughter speak like this before, or heard them express such hatred towards themselves and towards their parents. Parents may not only be shocked, but also quite frightened by the force of these emotions. It's important to stand firm and show that your love and support are solid. So do continue to offer a hug, even though you may be rejected. Try not to be frightened by the rages or let them overwhelm and defeat you. Although you will want to set some boundaries for extreme behaviour, let the anger go by and remember that the emotions are not directed against you personally, even though what your child may say or do can be very upsetting indeed.

PARENT TO PARENT

She became a different person – almost unrecognizable. She would tell us repeatedly that she was fat and hideous, had no friends – no one who cared – that she was so alone and despicable that she wanted to die, and deserved to die. Then she would run off, either to her room or sometimes out of the house and down the street, with one of us following her because we thought she might do something to herself or throw herself under a car. It was that scary.

Sometimes she'd bang the side of her head with her fists repeatedly and the blows made her cry out because they were so forceful. She even threw herself downstairs on quite a number of occasions. Once or twice on journeys back from appointments she'd try to get out of the car while I was still driving and everyone would scream. I thought my life had become a terrifying nightmare. I didn't know what to think or how to handle her and I was utterly terrified, as were my other children. I even imagined crashing the car to put an end to our misery.

When I tried to tell some of my friends, they just stared at me in disbelief or tried to make out that her behaviour was typical for teens. Well it wasn't, and their not understanding, or trying to pacify me, made me feel as if I'd exaggerated it. I felt completely alone.

We just tried to take the outbursts, to realize that it wasn't really her. She'd often be so apologetic afterwards and cry about it, wondering if we thought badly of her. We were just "wrung out" but tried to encourage her and ask her to explain her feelings, hoping to get her to understand her reactions a bit better. We just had to hug her and love her despite the awful rages and hope and pray they'd lessen, which, over time, they did.

We experienced probably the worst behaviour, and certainly the most aggressive outbursts directed at us, when she was on the weight restoring programme. Thankfully we had been warned to expect these outbursts around four to eight weeks into the programme.[8] She'd get quite violent – throwing things, swearing, and kicking, especially after she'd been weighed each week. She was also very moody most of the time and we weren't sure how to judge her mood as she often flew off the handle at the smallest comment.

We all "walked on eggshells" and let a lot go by, but we were encouraged to set some boundaries to this bad behaviour. We knew we had to allow her to let off steam, but we drew the line at physical violence toward us or the rest of the family. We told her if she needed to swear as badly as that then she'd have to go down the garden to do it. We thought that a punch bag might help, although she said she didn't use it. I think my husband got more use out of it! We did book her some riding lessons, which was a good non-aggressive way of getting rid of pent-up emotion. I secretly watched her groom and talk to her horse when I went to pick her up from the stables. They had a special relationship, which was quite therapeutic and provided her with a much-needed focus too.

Jane

? My son is lying to us about food and eating and I don't know how to deal with this.

When parents become aware that their child has been lying to them – especially about what they're eating, or rather not eating, when it's all so very important – then it's a terrible shock. If you've always brought up your child to be honest and to tell the truth then you not only feel deceived to find them lying, but also that you've failed and that the trust has gone between you. It is important to be vigilant and therefore wise to deceptions. You can calmly point out any major deceptions, while deciding to overlook others so as not to cause continual arguments. Lying about food and eating does not mean that your child has become a liar. It is a symptom of the eating disorder.

PARENT TO PARENT

It was really upsetting to hear him swear blindly he'd eaten lunch at his friend's house when I knew he hadn't. Of course, that was just the start. He lied about all sorts of things to do with food, not just what he'd eaten but why he hadn't had time to eat at school or about there being no milk left for cereal in the morning, or that he'd been too much in a rush to have any breakfast, that his dad didn't have any change for the school canteen. It went on and on – a string of lies. I felt I couldn't trust him any more and worse, that my hopes for him starting to eat normally again were crushed.

Then there were other deceptions. I could hardly believe that he'd put toast crumbs he'd collected from the toaster and scatter them on a plate and smear the edge with a bit of butter and jam to make it look as if he'd eaten toast. He would leave some cereal soaked in milk, just a bit in a bowl with a milky spoon sticking up in it, to make me believe he'd had his breakfast cereal. He'd also hide some of his meal up his sleeve or pretend to cough and dispose of food that way in his clenched fist. He'd sometimes store food in his cheeks.

It was all so dreadful, unbelievable, really, and I felt so stupid for being deceived. I felt very angry with him and threatened all sorts of punishments but they didn't seem to matter to him. It was as if his need to avoid food to lose weight was far more important to him than going on the internet or listening to music or anything else. He said he just didn't care. I thought about stopping his allowance but I didn't trust him not to steal – if not from me then perhaps from someone else. He'd always been a good boy but lately he'd become a different person.

The most upsetting moment was when we got back from the doctor's after he'd been weighed. It was quite early on when we were sure he had an eating problem and were trying to stop him from losing any more weight. The doctor said that he had stabilized and was quite pleased with him; I was very relieved. We were looking to future gains thinking that our efforts had been working and that we could overcome this.

When we got back I picked up his jacket to hang it in the cupboard. It was heavy and when I looked in the inside pockets there were stones in there, quite large ones too. I was stunned and so upset to think *that he'd purposely deceived the doctor and that his weight was actually lower and worse than we'd thought. I confronted my son about this, and was extremely vigilant from then on, wise to his tricks – or should I say the tricks of anorexia. My son also admitted to wearing gym weights under his trousers around his ankles when he was weighed, so we had to search him on weigh days, as if he was a prisoner; in a way he was.*

Sally

Check Point

The emotional effects of eating disorders on sufferers:

- Since eating disorders affect the mind, irrational and disturbed thinking and feelings will often be present.

- Self-harming (including self-poisoning) and suicidal tendencies often coexist with eating disorders.

- Eating disorders cause more deaths from suicide than any other psychiatric illness.

- Although self-harming is usually a coping method, sometimes it can be fatal by accident or because of the hopelessness of the sufferer.

? Our daughter talks of hearing voices and we're worried she's going "mad". Is this normal?

Most of us talk to ourselves from time to time – usually to encourage, remind, or gently scold ourselves – and this is quite normal. However, perpetual negative "self talk" is quite different and those with eating disorders can experience it acutely. If you are coping with this you may find it hard not to think that your child has become deranged, and often it isn't until parents have talked to us that they realize this is something that other parents face, that it is often a part of an eating disorder – anorexia particularly. This knowledge really does help them face the situation with a bit more courage and determination.

PARENT TO PARENT

She told us after some of her awful rages against her life and against us that she hears voices urging her to carry on with essentially a starvation diet. She would go for days without anything to eat at all, literally nothing. It was so hard for us to watch, and if she broke her resolve by eating the tiniest little piece of fruit then she'd get absolutely hysterical, throwing herself on to the floor, screaming, and crying. We'd never seen her behave like this. We were so upset.

On the one hand, of course, we were desperate for her to eat something, anything, because by that stage all thoughts of normal eating had disappeared and we were terrified that she'd collapse, forever mindful of what damage this might be doing to her. On the other hand, we knew that when she did eat the tiniest bit of anything then there would be "payback" and she'd insist that she had to be punished, that the voices were telling her that she was a failure, useless, a waste of space, and that she'd have to eat nothing for at least four days now to make up for having "given in".

We were advised to help her realize that the voice she heard was the voice of anorexia goading her and trying to force her to eat less and to lower her target constantly until it would consume her. I told her that anorexia was not her friend – that actually it wouldn't stop until she collapsed or lost her life. We knew we had to step in and not let it run its course, to remind her continually that she was strong, beautiful, loved, and had a future; that this terrible obsessive illness almost had a personality of its own if she recognized it as a friend. We told her it lied to her, which was true.

Jane

Check Point

The emotional effects of eating disorders on parents:

- The strain of caring and supporting can be responsible for parents' relationships being strained to the limits and beyond, even into separation and divorce.

- Parents and siblings need support and some require medication and counselling too.

- Your friends and family will probably want to help, so let them, especially with some practical things like a bit of ironing or housework.

She's so depressed as a result of not eating. How can we cope?

Sometimes clinical depression triggers an eating disorder, but depression is usually a consequence as well. Parents feel totally overwhelmed and worn out by the depression of their child. It's so difficult to withstand because it continues for so long and the constant negativity and hopelessness increase the child's resolve to eat less, so the depression makes some even more physically ill as well. You feel you've lost the child you once knew and may even be tempted unnecessarily to think this is your fault. You will need support and understanding from a few key people as you try to reassure, affirm, and motivate your child at home. They will need professional psychotherapy to address the emotional aspects of the eating disorder, and creative therapies can be extremely useful as well.

PARENT TO PARENT

Yes of course we all have times of being a bit low or down. Usually, though, there's a cause and one works through it, pretty swiftly in our house. We had seen some bleak and turbulent teenage times when my elder son was going through his mid-teens. During that time, everything we said seemed wrong and he communicated only by grunting and door slamming. But during our daughter's eating disorder years, it was on a different scale altogether.

The depression fuelled the illness and made her dependence on over-exercise and self-induced vomiting all the more strong. Of course the barrage of self-hatred was so hard to withstand because it was constant and it seemed as if nothing we said made any difference. All our logic, our encouragement, our considerable efforts to motivate her and get her involved with things, and the praise we gave her were either ignored or thrown back at us. It wore us down over many months and we didn't know how to respond and go forward.

We battled on with great difficulty. We found we could get little rest from the endless self-hatred and *arguing, and from her need for attention – reassurance as well as cuddles. She would argue with us about her size repeatedly so that eventually we learned to stop it. Instead of the "Yes, I am", "No you aren't!" pantomime, we found that if we gave her our **opinion** it meant that she couldn't tell us that we were wrong – they **were** our opinions. So, one of us would say "Well, I don't think you're all the things you say about yourself, even if you think them." If she tried to argue with that we would say, "No, that's not what I think and you can't know what I think", and that would end the argument.*

Even at night my wife would be up listening out for our daughter because she couldn't sleep; she would either come in to us or roam about downstairs. We were constantly worried about what she might do and so – although we were so exhausted – we barely slept for months. Often we had to have her sleep at the foot of our bed or in between us.

Our daughter did go on to receive specialist inpatient care for six months. It consisted of supervised eating and individual and group therapy, and we also attended family therapy sessions once a week. After-care was put in place with our local CAMHS, and once she was back at school she had a weekly outpatient session. Even though she had been back to normal weight for at least eight months, she told the consultant how hard she was finding life generally – and had always done.

We were surprised and very relieved to hear the consultant say that she thought our daughter would benefit from some anti-depressants as she felt that her depression and high anxiety should have been resolved by normal eating for the past eight months. She said it was likely that the anxiety and depression had pre-existed before the onset of the eating disorder.

Richard

ACTION PLAN

Managing your child's emotions

- Try not to be afraid of the emotions of your loved one.

- Recognize that your child is in a battle with his or her emotions and that the behaviour you find hurtful is not revealing the true nature of your child.

- Do get some professional therapeutic help for them.

- When your child is calmer, ask them if they recognize their emotions and whether they could talk to you about what they are feeling.

- Discuss with them ways of redirecting their feelings away from themselves and encourage alternative ways of getting rid of pent-up emotion.

- Keep them motivated and encourage them to look towards the future, reminding them of their personal qualities and their future despite their mood.

- Reassure your child that you love them, despite their emotional outpourings.

- Decide what acceptable bad behaviour under these circumstances is – and set limits.

- Do explain your tolerance of the emotional outbursts to other family members and your older relatives who may have different views on your handling of the situation.

- Be sensitive to the feelings of your other children and try to support them too. Watch out for them showing signs of unhappiness, unnecessary guilt, and even loss of appetite.

- Get some support for yourselves and talk to someone you trust.

- You will probably be overwhelmed by life and all that you have to do, so try to make a list of just a few main priorities then stick to these and leave out other tasks. This can really help you avoid mounting tension and stress.

- Do have faith that this is a passing phase and that a better ability to express their feelings more appropriately should follow.

- If you are worried that your child's emotions are becoming seriously out of control and you fear for their safety, then ring or see your doctor for advice – or talk to the professionals handling their care by telephone or in writing.

- Don't be afraid to call the emergency services if you fear for your child's mental safety.

CHAPTER 6

Managing Your Child's Behaviour

An eating disorder causes the sufferer to behave in ways that range from the bizarre to the appalling. Some of these you will have come across earlier in the book, but now we can focus on some of the most common behaviour associated with anorexia, bulimia, and binge-eating disorder and also with those disorders that cross the boundaries and overlap.

Since much of this type of behaviour is symptomatic of an eating disorder, you are unlikely to have witnessed it before or had experience trying to cope with your son or daughter constantly being sick, or hearing them jump up and down in secret in their room, for instance. How should you tackle your child's self-induced vomiting? What should you do about them over-using the gym or swimming pool, bingeing, taking laxatives or diet pills?

I was completely unprepared for my daughter making herself sick in addition to her anorexia and found it hard to deal with her behaviour and my feelings. Understandably, your first reaction is to try to stop the behaviour or lessen it somehow and to seek advice on how to prevent it from escalating. You also need some help and support with your own feelings. Friends and family, however kind and supportive, are also usually at a loss as to know how to help you and can be very shocked by what you are telling them. I certainly experienced this and found the reaction of others so difficult to take that I tried hard not to talk to anyone at all. As a result we all became isolated from other people, which was not good. I also hoped to receive more understanding and advice from professionals and felt unsupported at the time. So if you are facing terrible, and even terrifying, behaviour, then I can really understand that you might feel you have to struggle on without any resources or any help. If that is the case, then please contact ABC for support and look at the references at the back of this book for further help.

It's just so difficult for us to understand

Right now, you may wonder what you can do to help your child and whether there will ever be an end to this behaviour. The terrible thing is that many of these behaviours are designed to speed up weight loss, so even if your child is not at a dangerous weight you worry that they soon will be if this behaviour carries on. To you it defies all logic. It also defies your parenting. You can see so clearly where this will end and find it very hard to understand why they can't. Their behaviour is compulsive and obsessive, and your attempts to change it or to reason with them will be met with hostility or greater determination to hide it from you, but that doesn't mean that you shouldn't try.

There are additional behaviours associated with eating disorders that are particularly upsetting for parents and seem far removed from the norm, such as suicidal tendencies and self-harming, primarily in the form of cutting or burning. Personally, I can honestly say I felt completely unable to cope with these to begin with. I found it the most distressing thing I'd faced as a parent, something I never,

ever thought I'd have to deal with. Self-harm is very common among those suffering with eating disorders, and sufferers report that it helps them to feel in control and reduces feelings of panic about being out of control. For many, the act of self-harm begins as a way of expressing emotions that are overwhelming, confused, and cannot be put into words. Some use it to combat feelings of self-hatred and the desire to be thinner.

To begin with, parents find self-harming a terrible shock, and they fear that it may be an attempt on the part of their child to end their life, given that they have often voiced self-hatred. However, self-harming is not the same as having suicidal tendencies – though these can also occur in someone struggling with an eating disorder. Self-harm is usually an attempt to get some relief and to feel better. In contrast, suicide stems from a desire not to feel at all any more. However, sometimes self-harming can have unintentional fatal consequences. It is also important to state that many of the lives that are lost to an eating disorder are due to suicide.

Once the initial shock that your son or daughter self-harms, threatens suicide, or may even attempt it, has lessened, you will want to know how you can get help for them urgently and support them through to recovery. If you experience this type of behaviour and recognize something of your situation in the following parent experiences, then I hope that it will also encourage you to seek professional help if you have not already done so.

- -

DID YOU KNOW?
FACTS ABOUT YOUR WELL-BEING

- *Managing difficult behaviour is a huge strain for parents. They get little rest, even at night, and are permanently on edge either waiting for the next occurrence or responding to a crisis – taking verbal abuse, being hit or spat at – trying to keep the child they love safe whilst also protecting the rest of the family and the home. Being in a permanent state of alert is very tiring and not having an end in sight is debilitating.*

Getting some respite, even taking a bath or stepping out into the fresh air, is sometimes all parents are able to do to help themselves recover a little.

- *The pressure of continuously coping with your child's very negative emotions such as depression, the compulsion to self-harm, and suicidal tendencies (which often go hand in hand with an eating disorder), means that you are likely to struggle with stress. Stress has serious consequences for your physical health: insomnia, frequent headaches and migraine, chest pains, panic attacks, and depression are all common.*

- *The effects of your child's eating disorder can also be seen on your relationships with others: your partner, your children, other family members, and your friends. You do need to seek help for yourself to keep you sane, physically well, and strong enough to look after the child with the eating disorder and your family.*

- -

? How do we stop our daughter from being sick after meals?

To begin with, parents often consider trying to prevent their child from being sick after meals as the obvious-looking solution to the problem. They also try distraction techniques such as going out for a walk or playing a game together after a meal, which can help a little. However, the problem goes deeper and the self-induced vomiting, laxative or diet pill abuse, and compulsive exercise are really symptoms of the issues that need to be addressed during professional treatment and by certain self-help exercises.

Self-help suggestions include keeping a record of events and feelings – for instance, before the urge to be sick. After a period of time, when looking back over the entries, trigger factors can be identified. This can help someone to understand some of the reasons for the things they do, which in turn can help them begin to avoid certain circumstances or minimize the severity of their emotional responses. Eventually these kinds of practical exercises can help someone overcome their eating disorder, especially when combined with professional talking therapies, particularly Cognitive Behavioural Therapy (CBT). In very general terms CBT's approach helps someone to identify their thoughts and feelings and to relate them to their behaviour in order to make changes.

PARENT TO PARENT

Our early efforts consisted of lots of threats and lectures about how being sick could cause a heart attack or bleeding in the throat. We read up on all the medical consequences and thought that if we bombarded her with all the health risks then she'd be frightened into stopping. We found that it didn't work and actually made her more upset and anxious – more unable to cope, more unable to eat, more likely to be sick. In fact we noticed that she was able to be sick rather randomly, not because she'd eaten and then gone to the bathroom, but just sick suddenly, wherever she was, through stress and the terrible atmosphere in our house: me shouting, my wife crying, and neither of us knowing how to approach her normally any more.

We had got to a stage where we didn't know if it was better if she didn't eat – that way she wouldn't need to be sick. We were totally confused mentally as to whether eating was good or bad. We were also inconsistent to begin with, and I realized that my wife and I had different approaches to our daughter, which didn't help at all.

We found that what did help her was to get her some counselling and to agree to reinforce the approach of the counsellor together at home. She

*was really marvellous and gave us all a private
slot with her where she was able to coordinate the
support without betraying my daughter's confidence.
If you like, she coached us. We continued to provide
normal food and encouraged our daughter to eat
enough and not to go too long on an empty stomach,
because we knew that she'd be prone to bingeing
otherwise. By having the counsellor to lean on and
to offload some of the severe tension and anger, we
were calmer and we took the opportunity to listen
to our daughter and to try to see the eating disorder
from her point of view.*

*We were advised to help our daughter record her
feelings around food and mealtimes, and to match
them with what had gone on during the day. Then
she could begin to see why certain events or the
feelings around them triggered the desire either not
to eat or to eat voraciously and then be sick. It was
long, painstaking work and of course there were
days when she got angry and wanted to give up.
There were times when we were exhausted with it,
but it did help her to understand what she was doing
as well as to understand her feelings (previously
confusion, fear, and deep distress).*

Richard

? What do I do about my son's over-exercising?

Obsessive exercise is really hard to deal with. It seems obvious to
parents, their friends, and family that the person struggling with
an eating disorder would not want to exercise owing to feeling
weak and experiencing constant headaches and tiredness. Parents
feel torn about stopping exercise as it might appear to their child
as if they are punishing them. They may think they can just stop
their child exercising, only to find that they can't and that others

criticize them for it. It isn't that easy, of course, particularly if your child exercises in secret or out of your sight. For someone with low weight, or with a potential heart risk, it is vital to curb exercise, and you will probably need the help of their school or college as well as a doctor's note or consultant's written instruction to back this up.

PARENT TO PARENT

We did stop his football, saying that we'd reinstate it once he was at a better weight, but to begin with we spoke to his sports teachers at school. They suggested having him as a sub and interchanging him for a short period with other players because they didn't want him to be singled out. He loved sport and to begin with none of us wanted to take away from him the one thing he really enjoyed. It seemed as if we were punishing him.

We then tried using sport as a reward for eating better and it did help to begin with. We used the "energy in, energy out" analogy (rather like the way a car needs to be refuelled in order to run), but there came a time when he was completely unable to see reason and would do circuits and jogging behind our backs. He would make excuses for going out and we would ground him. The arguments about this were really fierce, but the school was very good and they backed us up telling him that they couldn't take the risk of him collapsing during a sports lesson and that he'd have to sit and watch, or go to the library or to the school nurse. That was a great relief to me, although it didn't help with secret exercise in his room or his using exercise DVDs when we were out.

Julia

? My daughter gets on the scales several times a day. What should I do?

You may or may not notice an obsession with the scales. Using the scales daily or repeatedly throughout the day is to be avoided because body weight fluctuates throughout the day by a kilogramme or so. Of course, clothes account for some extra weight during the day as well. Once a child sees their weight and it appears greater than they thought, it fuels the desire to eat less and produces even greater anxiety and self-hatred. Approach this first by removing the scales from the bathroom or any other accessible place and putting them out of sight. If your child has anorexia then you may need to record their weight at home, in which case weighing is usually advised on a weekly basis.

PARENT TO PARENT

I hadn't realized she was doing this and so I felt really stupid and guilty that I hadn't thought that this might be going on. No one uses the scales much in our house and they don't feature in our lives. She had told me her weight and so I presumed she'd used the scales. I didn't want to challenge her so I removed the batteries from the scales hoping that would stop her but she must have bought new batteries because the scales started to work again. So I hid the scales wondering if she'd say anything, which she did, in quite a rage. I was really shocked at just how much she relied on knowing her weight all through the day.

We talked, eventually more calmly, and I realized that she was setting herself a weight target that was too low for her and that this target decreased as soon as she got to it. She told me she weighed herself after everything she ate or drank and if her weight on the scales was slightly higher than her morning weight then she would be inconsolable and determined to lower the target. She couldn't understand that sometimes it was just only a glass of water that had made a difference to her weight, and when I pointed this out she said that she'd have to give up water. She agreed that water had no calories, but because her weight changed all she could surmise was that the nutritional information was a lie. It was an extremely difficult period for me as she lost weight, became dehydrated and was totally obsessed with the scales.

I suggested taking charge of the scales and that supervised by me she was weighed every other day to begin with, getting down to weekly at the doctor's or at the eating disorders unit once her referral had come through. To start with she was dreadful on the days she wasn't allowed the scales because she was so frightened she'd put on masses of weight and, as a result, she tried to eat less. I knew I couldn't get her better at home and that I was just trying to contain her illness. Once the professional help began she agreed to them weighing her once a week as part of her weight-restoring programme.

Towards the end of her treatment she tried hard not to be so dependent on the scales and preferred to get on backwards so that only the staff knew her weight. Once home, her doctor saw the weight, but it was important for her to be weighed each week in order to reassure her that her weight was on target and not more. This went on for a long time, but now she's back to a normal weight she doesn't use scales at all. She feels it's better for her not to know her weight. She just relies on her clothes to remind her that she's the right size, as she still struggles to *see herself realistically and is prone to stress about being "huge" from time to time even though she's so slim.*

Anne

Check Point

Information about extreme and shocking behaviour in those with eating disorders:

- Dependence on the scales and using the scales several times a day in order to check weight increases the fear of weight gain and makes re-establishing normal eating more difficult.

- Anxiety fuels an eating disorder and can increase dependence on self-harm, therefore your reactions – any anger, nagging, or ridicule – will only serve to increase their reliance on self-harm and the eating disorder.

- Remember that the eating disorder began as a coping mechanism and when it is starting to be withdrawn and replaced, panic, confusion, and fear spill out into very difficult behaviour.

? How do we cope with self-harm?

Discovering self-harm is a huge shock for parents and is intensely worrying because parents often mistakenly think the coping strategy that cutting, biting, or burning provides is the same as an attempt at suicide. If your child is young and still lives at home you will need to be watchful and try to put obvious methods of harming, such as sharp knives, razor blades, and paracetamol, out of reach. However it's impossible to make your home completely free of objects a child intent on self-harm could use. Talking with your child without anger, disgust, horror, or too much emotion, so that you allow them to tell you a little of what they are feeling, is a good start. Some parents find that their child's initial attempts at self-harming don't develop into a serious problem, however if this is not the case then you'll want to find some professional help for them. The support and understanding you provide will also be very important for their recovery from self-harm and you will need to help them treat or care for any injuries.

PARENT TO PARENT

We burst through the bathroom door because we were so concerned about the emotional state of our daughter. I found her sitting fully clothed in an empty bath holding her dad's razor. I was stunned and utterly terrified – so too my other daughters. I'd never heard of self-harm and I couldn't believe that she could ever want to do anything to herself.

To realize that she was in such emotional distress was terrible. I didn't know what to do and was in a state of shock. I rang my doctor, who was brilliant. She told me to remember that I was in charge, which helped me back into the parental role and was a great help. She also told me to take all the obvious sharp objects, and any paracetamol tablets, and lock them away. We couldn't make our home completely free of any potential objects for harming, but at least it felt that we were doing something to help prevent it and to avoid temptation.

We were obviously vigilant from then on and we spent time with our daughter trying to encourage her to talk to us about it, so we could understand a bit better why she felt the need to do this. We found a good, experienced local counsellor with whom we could all work, and learned to help our daughter gradually develop some different strategies to cope and express her feelings and emotions.

Jane

Check Point

Further information about extreme and shocking behaviour in those with eating disorders:

- Remember that those who self-harm do so because they want to make sense out of the confusion and pain they are feeling, and not to seek attention. In fact, most are deeply ashamed and therefore they self-harm in places that are hard to see in order for it to be kept secret.

- If your child suffers with "multi-impulsive bulimia" it means that, in addition to the cycle of restricting eating (leading to bingeing and then to purging), alcohol and/or drug abuse and wild behaviour (even including promiscuity and shoplifting) can be part of the condition and people suffering really do experience severe loss of control.

- Trying to bring those behaving in this way back into some form of control and providing some strategies to help is essential – alongside professional management.

? How can we cope with OCD, overdoses, and threatened suicide?

Obsessive Compulsive Disorder (OCD)[9] is an anxiety disorder that can trigger eating difficulties and even eating disorders. Sustained high anxiety and fear can lead sufferers to want to withdraw from life. So OCD can be really hard to live with and supporting someone means that you will need to ask for the help of experienced professionals if your child is under sixteen years old. If they are older, then hopefully you can persuade or guide them towards seeking professional help for themselves. Threatened suicide should always be taken seriously and any overdoses followed up straight away. If in doubt, don't hesitate to call an ambulance immediately, as speed is of the essence in dealing with this situation.

PARENT TO PARENT

To begin with the manifestations were easy enough to cope with. She would ask us to move things in her bedroom that were touching each other and we'd explain to her that things couldn't catch fire without any ignition as she imagined. We gave her time and a lot of reassurance for her worries and tried reasoning. When she was young, her worst OCD came in the form of constant hand washing, but it didn't last too long and we didn't think to get professional help. Later, once the eating disorder had taken a hold, the anxiety and OCD intensified and started to affect her mind in more ways than before. She became so anxious just from living life generally, and saw danger everywhere. She needed an escape, I suppose. We found her talking about not wanting to carry on living any more and, after a particularly stressful day of exams following a huge build-up due to her own expectations, she attempted suicide with an overdose of paracetamol, which she'd been storing unbeknown to us.

We rushed her to hospital, as we knew how serious this could be, especially as she was at a low weight. After that, we found it hard not to fear for her safety each day. It was a case of being with her as often as we could, attempting to encourage her, watching out for signs, and hoping that the professional treatment she was receiving for her eating disorder would restore her mind. Gradually it did, though not without unbelievable suffering to us all.

Richard

ACTION PLAN

Managing your child's behaviour

- Set some boundaries for bad behaviour, but allow your child to vent some of their feelings and anguish as it is beneficial to their recovery.

- Seek professional advice and support for yourselves and for them.

- Be on the lookout for obsessive and compulsive exercise.

- You will need to curb – or even stop – sports, exercise, or walking to and from school if your child is at a low weight.

- You may need to arrange time off for them from school or college in order to conserve their energy.

- Keep bathroom scales under your supervision. Keep them hidden or locked away in between the designated times for weighing your child.

- Don't ignore self-harm or be angry, but encourage them to talk to you about it and work towards understanding it and reducing the occurrences.

- If you stay shocked, disgusted, or angry then your child will find it impossible to seek your help.

- You may need to remove some of the most obviously harmful items (such as paracetamol, razor blades, and sharp knives) and be vigilant and alert to episodes of self-harming.

- Explore other methods of coping and ask your child what helps them. It could be diversionary tactics, or talking, or being held, or sleeping.

- Clean and check any wounds and look out for those that your child might be keeping hidden such as cuts or burns on the stomach or just under the pant line.

- If necessary, get them medical attention for any wounds or injuries.

- Don't be afraid to call the emergency services if you fear for your child's safety.

- As you will experience severe stress, do try to get some rest when you can and find support for yourself.

CHAPTER 7

Finding and Receiving Treatment

When you are struggling against an eating disorder that seems not only to have overtaken your child, but also the whole family and your life, then treatment is something that you long for. However that treatment can often seem mysterious and facing it for the first time can be quite intimidating, causing additional fear and anxiety. The treatment process that you hope will help bring the person you love through to recovery will be unfamiliar to you. Knowing what is available and the stages of treatment that your child may go through will hopefully reassure you as it will help you know what to expect.

By reading about the treatment process that I and other parents accessed with our children, I hope you will also realize that although, as one parent put it, "We seemed to live a parallel existence, in completely uncharted waters, seeing psychiatrists and psychologists through a haze of our own exhaustion and misery", we did get through the various treatment processes outlined and on to recovery. Not everyone needs to go through all the treatments described by parents in this chapter. Various factors determine what is offered or needed – notably the age of the patient, their physical and mental health, the part of the country where you live, and what services are thought to be in the patient's best interests at the time.

Giving your child into another's care

One of the hardest things I found about inpatient treatment – apart from the fear of what it comprised – is the complete handing over of your extremely ill child to a programme of treatment with an uncertain outcome: letting others take over where you may feel you've failed. Along with this sense of failure, the feeling of "handing over" goes against your instinct to care for someone who has become very emotionally dependent on you and who is usually refusing to co-operate with treatment. You're faced with having to think with your head and not your heart, knowing that you've taken their care as far as you can. You may have been battling the eating disorder for months – or even years – doing everything in your power to stop it, coping largely unaided with all those mealtimes, emotions, and health deterioration. But now you realize that your efforts have to be superseded by others with more experience in eating disorders in order to give your child the best possible chance of recovery. Now, although you will still be strongly involved and supportive, it's in their best interests for you to hand over their care to professionals.

I so understand the tears and the agony of parents who tell me that their child has had to go away for inpatient care and may have been begging not to go. I remember having to prise my daughter out of the wardrobe in which she was hiding and then out of the car and into hospital with all her tears and protestations. The separation of parent and child is often extremely painful because the child's emotional dependence on the parent has become so deep-rooted. The illness is not purely a physical one which makes the handing over much harder.

Some parents have to take the incredibly difficult step of agreeing for their adult child to be sectioned under the Mental Health Act or, as I did, of taking their child to hospital because of the threat of heart attack, chest pains, extreme self-harming, or even overdosing. Other parents have been longing for more comprehensive care while trying to help their child at home for a very long time before a referral is made. They may find they are then on a waiting list for what seems like an eternity.

Then, of course, there's the understandable fear as to whether or not treatment will work. Most parents want treatment to be the cure for the eating disorder. However, if you can, try to think of it as a part of the journey towards recovery. That journey consists of improvements to your child's physical health and the restoration of their mental health through therapy, with any trigger factors being examined and dealt with. It also consists of improving their attitude towards themselves and towards food, practical changes in their eating, and ultimately both they and you enjoying life again.

DID YOU KNOW?
FACTS ABOUT TREATMENT

- *Children under sixteen years of age can be made to receive treatment if their parents and medical team think it's in their best interest.*

- *Children of fifteen and sixteen have the right to confidentiality and a say in their treatment.*

- *Children over the age of sixteen are allowed to refuse treatment for an eating disorder.*

- *Those who refuse treatment can be sectioned under the Mental Health Act if their life is in danger and they lack the capacity to decide their care. Sectioning requires a team of approved mental health providers – for example a social worker, doctor, or psychiatrist – and next of kin.*

❓ What professional help is available and how do we access it?

The service offered by the NHS in England, Scotland, and Northern Ireland is divided into the Child and Adolescent Mental Health Service (CAMHS) and the Adult Eating Disorder Service for those over eighteen years of age. Your child's doctor will make the referral to one of these services. It is via these eating disorder services that your child will see a consultant psychiatrist, a psychologist, eating disorder nurses and dieticians, and family therapists. To begin with this will be as an outpatient, but if necessary inpatient care may be offered. If you are worried that your child is dangerously ill physically – for instance if they experience chest pains, frequently faint, have a very low BMI and are still regularly losing more than a 500 g (1 lb) a week, or if they are very depressed or hopeless and you fear for their emotional state, then you may need to call an ambulance or drive them to Accident and Emergency.

PARENT TO PARENT

We coped as best we could for several months, seeing the doctor and trying to manage our daughter's anorexia, but we could see that mentally, the illness had "changed gear" and she was far less rational and less able to fight it.

Also her low weight, which we were so terrified about, was getting even lower and although I kept on taking her back to the doctor, I think even he didn't know what more we could both do. The doctor said that her BMI [see Appendix 1 for an explanation] was now low enough for her to be in the severe anorexic band and that he'd put in for urgent referral to the CAMHS for our daughter to be assessed in the next week, with a view to their taking over her care. The words "psychiatrist" and "mental health" really unnerved me. I hadn't thought that my daughter had a mental illness and I felt quite shocked. Obviously I just had to get past that. It was good to ask my doctor questions about the future treatment on offer and he explained it quite well. He said that the assessment would also contain some questionnaires about self-perception and of course they'd weigh her, calculate her BMI, and continue to do medical tests.

He said that, to begin with, the consultant would probably see her once a fortnight or once a week. They might then ask her to take her meals at their unit once a week prior to giving her an inpatient place if she lost more weight or became more depressed and unable to make any improvements. With regard to the question of school, the consultant might put her on half days or at least a reduced timetable in order to preserve her energy. The doctor also told me that she'd receive individual therapy and that we'd all have family therapy once a fortnight. This might be multi-family therapy where more than one family would be attending and sharing.

It was all quite a shock but at least I knew what was coming. My daughter was desperate not to go into hospital or into inpatient specialist care and her consultant used this to try to get her to work with him over the weeks that followed. It was good to have him behind us, someone checking on her and who had set a target weight for her below which he said he wouldn't let her go.

Jane

? We've been told we're to receive family therapy but don't know what to expect and I'm worried. How do other parents find this?

Parents often fear family therapy as intrusive or something that might cast blame on them. Many long for family therapy because they think it exists to help both the parents and children in the family – and usually they all need it. Its primary aim, though, is to help us understand anorexia, bulimia, and binge eating and to get everyone working together to help the child with the eating disorder recover so that the family is happy and united again. Of course, family therapy is therefore useful for a range of other issues besides eating disorders, such as bereavement, coming to terms with cancer, anxiety disorders, agoraphobia, and autism spectrum disorders.

Try as hard as possible not to be frightened of going to family therapy and aim to establish a good relationship with your therapist. Also remember that it is important to allow your child some space within the session to say how they are feeling. Don't be worried if they don't talk at all at first – hopefully that will come later. If you have other children, they will probably be invited along. Although they may be worried about missing school, what to say, whether or not they are to be blamed, it is good to have the whole family supporting the child with the eating disorder, and their attendance at every session is not usually compulsory.

Parent to Parent

We longed for our first session of family therapy. We thought it would instantly give us comfort and strategies and we were disappointed after the first few sessions, to be honest. It did give my other children the opportunity to say how they felt about her illness, but actually most of the time they were bored with talking about it. They didn't have to go each time but when they did they were encouraged to do drawings if they didn't want to speak. I think the therapist got quite a lot of information about their feelings and about relationships in the family from those drawings.

We were very hopeful to begin with, and then we found that our son just wouldn't talk at all and we despaired of ever coming through this. He seemed just as angry and sullen as before. The sessions made my husband and me row quite a bit, too, as we felt we were being judged, and also we disagreed with each other about how to approach our son; this came out in the therapy meetings.

My husband was quite dictatorial, thinking it was a slur on his parenting, and I was probably a bit too soft and let our son's illness get the better of me. We had plenty of arguments in the car going back from the sessions, which was pretty ghastly at the time. But during the week we both thought back on what had been said and I think we used it. It was hard not to think we were being "tripped up" and blamed for causing the eating disorder, but the therapist reassured us that it wasn't about blame – it was about us all working as a team to see off this eating disorder and to keep it from returning. He told us we were our son's most powerful allies and said we had a big part to play in his recovery. He helped us not to be frightened of our son whilst he was in the grip of this illness. We felt encouraged to believe in ourselves as a family, which wasn't perfect – but then, whose is?

Sue

Check Point

Some of the concerns parents have about treatment:

- You will doubtless be very anxious about inpatient care if it has been suggested, and amongst other things may worry about your child learning new tricks and extreme behaviour from other patients. Remember, however, that many patients are very supportive of others and a good unit will be wise to the behaviours symptomatic of an eating disorder. However, if you feel your child is being influenced by others then talk to the staff.

- An adult child refusing help may need your intervention or that of emergency medical services in order to treat them.

? My daughter has been admitted to hospital. What will happen?

Children are usually admitted to a children's ward of a general hospital if their physical health is of concern. You may hope that their eating disorder is treated straight away, but it is more usual to find that in a general hospital they are simply kept safe and monitored, for instance, by keeping them on bed rest and observation. Their blood pressure will be monitored at regular intervals and they may need to be weighed often. They could be seen by psychiatric staff and by the hospital dietician. Further tests may be done, such as blood tests and sometimes heart checks, for example an ECG. If a child is very low in weight, feeding via a nasogastric tube may be considered, and some children require a drip to help restore fluids. A child who is very ill may then be transferred to a more specialized environment for treatment, for instance an Eating Disorder Unit in the county, or further away to a specialist hospital or clinic. Here they should receive medical care and therapy alongside practical help with eating. They may have to stay for several months until their weight and emotional state are restored sufficiently for them to return home. After-care should be put in place before they leave a specialist unit so that a local consultant oversees their progress once home.

PARENT TO PARENT

Our daughter was admitted to hospital because her heartbeat had dropped to thirty-three, which was half the output for her age. She was also dehydrated because she had lost water through vomiting and laxative abuse. She hardly drank anything either at that stage. We were terrified that she'd die. We'd wanted her to receive more intensive treatment for a long time and felt we'd been playing an agonizing waiting game, knowing that something terrible like this would probably happen.

There had been times when my partner suggested I take her to A&E, and I would have done so if she'd got any worse or, of course, if she'd collapsed. I'd been advised to look out for chest pains and fainting as well as her mood, which had been very black with talk of suicide. Her consultant at the Eating Disorder Unit rang to say he'd admitted her to a general ward for rest and observation. I felt so relieved that she'd be safe there. I'd been beside myself with worry and in a terrible state for the past couple of weeks. It was like living with a ticking bomb.

She wasn't allowed to get out of bed. She had

been given an ECG to see how her heart was coping with the strain brought about by the eating disorder. They had done the usual blood tests to check her electrolyte balance to see if her heart was OK. They wanted to talk to us about nasogastric tube feeding. We didn't know much about this and I was really worried. They told me that unless she began to eat and they could see a rise in her daily weight chart, then they would need to get some food and vital nutrients into her by this means. They'd already put her on a fluids drip. It was good to have my partner there, not only for moral support, but also to remind me of things I'd forgotten to ask.

The sister explained that psychiatrically trained nurses would administer the tube just in case she were to resist and that they would probably give her a sedative first. The tube feed contained all the necessary calories and nutrients and she would stay on it until her weight was out of the danger zone. They told me that once her health was more stable they'd transfer her to a unit that specialized in eating disorders – thankfully an adolescent one because it wouldn't be right to have her in an adult unit. Here she'd receive therapy and learn to eat normally again.

She threatened to pull out the nasogastric tube – but didn't thankfully – and it was successful in putting the required kilogrammes on her, even though she cried and complained about the weight gain and said that once she was out of hospital she'd lose all that weight again. That was an extremely upsetting threat, but no more than that.

Helen

Check Point

Further concerns some parents have about treatment:

• You may be worried about your child's care, their mood, or their behaviour. If so you can, discuss your concerns with one of the nurses in charge or with your doctor.

• If you feel unhappy about any aspects of the treatment – for instance if it is suggested that your child is to be placed on an adult ward or tube-fed without your agreement or against their will – then do make your views known.

• Forced feeding is very different from nasogastric feeding and should not be permitted, so do ask first what methods will be used and raise any concerns as early as possible.[10]

? We're without advice or any kind of action plan. What should we do?

Outpatient care and inpatient care involve teams of professionals including nursing staff, dieticians, psychologists, and psychiatrists. When everything is going well you will have the care of your child co-ordinated between all these professionals and a good aim and care-plan will be outlined for you. If you don't understand the approach your team is taking, or if you don't feel included in your child's care, especially if they are living at home, then it's always a good idea to ask to speak to someone in charge. This is a highly worrying stage so it's not unusual to feel anxious and frustrated. Your team should understand your feelings, but it's wise to try to stay calm and to keep good relationships with them.

PARENT TO PARENT

I expected the hospital staff to be able to treat the eating disorder when, in hindsight, I probably should have realized that they were concentrating on her medical condition, but I was so alarmed that she was losing weight, despite all the care she was receiving and the input of the hospital dietician. Of course, our daughter was being just as defiant as she was at home and the illness hadn't loosened its grip on her. I suppose I had naively thought that once she was in hospital she'd get better.

I have to say that I was terrified of losing her and I hadn't been prepared for her condition to worsen. We were at the hospital every day, with me rushing there after work, often totally exhausted. My wife would have had the emotions of our daughter to cope with all day, together with the normal school run for our other children and seeing to their needs. She would now be looking imploringly at me to do something and to take charge.

Nobody seemed able to tell us what they proposed to do. I think I came across as very angry, but I don't cry. I had to hold it all together for everyone, so I guess my emotions came out in another way. The hospital staff suspected that I might have been angry or abusive to my daughter at home. My wife managed to explain why I was behaving like this, even though her emotions often got the better of her as well. We made an appointment to speak with the consultant, actually asking him to discuss her case, the approach they were taking, and what they'd be doing next. We felt as if no one was communicating with us. Once we'd had the meeting we felt a lot more positive. We wanted to work with them and be directed by them. After all, they had the expertise that we wanted to learn.

David

ACTION PLAN

Finding and receiving treatment

- Stay in touch with your family doctor, even if your child is receiving more specialist care, so he or she can monitor their situation and give you some support, perhaps signposting you to a counsellor or a support group.

- Try to keep communication open between you and your child's consultant and the rest of the team involved in their treatment.

- If you feel you haven't received a care plan or that you don't understand the options or the approach they are taking towards it, then ask your professionals for information.

- If your child is unsure about accepting treatment, particularly if they are an adult, help them to gain as much information about what it will comprise and where it will take place.

- If your child is referred to a specialized Eating Disorders Unit, look it up together on the internet or see if you can visit beforehand and maybe even meet one or two key members of staff.

- Talk with your child about the future benefits of accepting treatment and put some incentives into place.

- If they are an adult, help them with practical matters such as arranging when you can visit, finding out what needs doing at their home, and helping to manage their affairs.

If they are younger, help them to carry on with their school or college work. Worry about these things might be an obstacle to their accepting treatment.

- Help them stay occupied while they are in hospital, for example with art work, games, magazines, or hobbies.

- Help them to feel loved, supported, encouraged, and not forgotten. Arrange visits from friends, cards and letters, photographs, and their own duvet cover or some other reminders of home.

- Make sure an after-care plan is put in place before your child is discharged from a hospital or specialized unit.

- The period of inpatient care can often be like a grieving period for parents when, suddenly, after all your caring and hard work, your child is taken away from you. Do get some extra support and allow yourself some time to recover.

CHAPTER 8

Going Through to Recovery

As we saw in the last chapter, treatment is often a very important part of recovery, but it is not the only part. Indeed your child might not require comprehensive treatment or might even refuse it. Here we'll be looking at questions about recovery and about how to get your child through an eating disorder and back to normality. We'll look at maintaining recovery in the following chapter but, for now, let's focus on what recovery is all about. We'll look at the experience of recovery, including my own and that of some of ABC's parents and their children, which will demonstrate how you can play an extremely important role in the recovery of your child.

Recovery – is it *really* possible?

First, it's very important for you to hang on to the fact that recovery from an eating disorder – a real and lasting one – is possible, despite what you may have heard. I can tell you that recovery is achievable even against all the odds – through the worst physical and emotional experiences. I can maintain this with confidence, not just because of my own experience and the experience of the many parents ABC has supported whose children have gone on to recover, but also because of the many recovered sufferers themselves we have supported. A number of these sufferers were adults and their parents therefore played a supportive role, rather than a driving one.

It's important that you believe in recovery for your child and that you convey this belief to them – in fact that you keep this hope alive for them while they are too weak or depressed to own it themselves. Part of the problem for sufferers is not being able to understand what recovery really is or to accept that it is achievable. Unless they are helped, their attempts to do so may well be futile. Many sufferers are perfectionists, so if they fear that recovery is not possible unless it is done perfectly and in a certain way, they may not risk defeat by trying. This is why it is so important for you to understand what recovery looks like, to carry on encouraging them, and to keep believing in it.

The usual definition of recovery focuses on "being back to normal". Of course, for many people with an eating disorder, this brings to mind thoughts of having to go back to how they felt before – distressed and unhappy, but now having "lost" the option of "coping" with this by controlling their weight. You can therefore see why, to many sufferers, the concept of "recovery" is a difficult one, and why your understanding of it and your steadfast encouragement is so vital.

Naturally, you'll have times, as I did, when you wonder whether your child will recover at all, or whether the progress you are seeing really is the beginning of permanent recovery, but do try to share the understandable worry and heartache with the people supporting you and not with your child.

- -

DID YOU KNOW?
FACTS ABOUT RECOVERY

- *Yes, of course, recovery is about weight gain or stabilization, and about bingeing or purging being a thing of the past; and these may have to be urgently addressed before any other support or therapy can be offered if they are causing serious physical harm. However, recovery is more than this. Recovery is a process; one that addresses the reasons why food is being used as a coping method, and how a sufferer sees themselves and their life.*

- *Recovery is not always a forward path and there are usually many backward steps. But though these are terribly hard to go through, they actually strengthen progress. Recovery is about your child learning to view things differently and accepting help to find new strategies that work for them. Some of these will be to do with food and eating, others will be about their emotional responses to life and involve their thinking, feelings, and communication, so that ultimately freedom from disordered thinking and behaviour can be achieved.*

- -

? What is recovery?

Parents want their child to recover completely and for this recovery to happen quickly. Some are desperate for them to be back to a healthy weight because they are so frightened of their being at risk physically. Others want the obsession about size and the difficulties surrounding food, eating, and exercise to be over; the destructive behaviour and emotional torment to be things of the past. However, recovery is not a fast return to normal. Instead it is a journey towards freedom from the constraints of disordered eating and many, if not all, of its consequences. The journey, which may or may not involve treatment, may last many months, if not years.

PARENT TO PARENT

I wanted it all to be over and for her to be relaxed and happy again. The eating disorder put a long and terrible strain on our whole family, sucking the joy and humour right out of us, and so we hated living with it. I spent a lot of time being upset, frightened, and exhausted. Because we lurched from one crisis to the next with misery, anger, and resentment in between, we couldn't take the opportunity to think further ahead – about recovery in its widest sense.

Her physical health meant that she needed urgent medical treatment in hospital and then a transfer to a specialist unit for three months where her weight was restored. Real recovery took place afterwards. It was about her learning to cope in different ways rather than by restricting her eating, and to think less critically of herself – to accept herself and to take a few small risks, and to be less confused and hesitant about everything generally.

She'd been restored to normal weight in the unit but now she was managing to add a small snack of her choosing, then, little by little, adding quantity, not being consumed by guilt, and then expanding the range of foods she felt comfortable trying.

To begin with, all these positives seemed like a few glimpses of progress that we could hardly bear to believe would last, but then more were added and these achievements grew. She certainly did it her way. Just as she had let the eating disorder into her life, she was now deciding to make changes to see it off, and I think that was powerful for her as again it was in her control. We saw her begin to take new opportunities at school and also take an interest in

127

some of her old hobbies once again, abandoning some for new ones. As her psychiatrist remarked, she was "choosing life over anorexia".

We had read about motivation and helping a sufferer to try to imagine their life without the eating disorder by writing down a list of pros and cons. Her therapist was also working with her on this, so she'd try to think not only about what the eating disorder provided, but also what it had taken from her. Her health had obviously suffered and she'd lost some opportunities with friendships and some schoolwork through all the absences at outpatient meetings and during inpatient care. We knew that she was looking towards the next five years, answering the question of whether the eating disorder would have taken more from her than it provided in five years' time. Some of the motivational questions, such as about having a family, were too far away to make any impact because she was too young.

She said that it was her daily existence that got her down the most. She had realized for herself that the misery, the hunger, all the appointments, and the limits anorexia placed on her life made her feel imprisoned and she was prepared to take the chance to get out. She wanted to be normal and free.

Jane

❓ How long does recovery take?

This is one of the most frequently asked questions, the answer to which parents long for. Unfortunately there is no definitive timescale, although some clinicians talk about five years of sustained recovery, with relapses being more common in the first year. Recovery depends on a number of factors, notably the length and severity of the illness, the rapport between the child and the professionals working with them, the treatment they do or don't receive, support from family, friends, school, college, or work, and their own determination and hard work towards it. Although the process of recovery seems long, especially when you are facing uncertainty and having to cope, day in, day out, you will find that you will see glimpses of progress which begin to add up to achievements. You will notice your child's attitudes and behaviour beginning to change for the better, and the time spent in recovery becomes easier as it goes along.

PARENT TO PARENT

I wouldn't say her recovery took place in the Eating Disorders Unit, although it was there that her weight restoration took place, together with more intense individual therapy. Of course that was part of her recovery and without it I don't believe she could have gone on to full recovery. However, even when she was back to a normal weight and discharged from there, she was still not recovered, and by that I mean her mind was still that of someone with anorexia. To begin with, a large part of her conversation at home was about wanting to be thin again and she talked of how she could one day achieve that, knowing that her father and I wouldn't let her eating slip while she was still at home and while a new therapist took over. This is what she said about it:

"Coming home from the unit where I'd had to gain weight back to my normal weight for height and age was one of the hardest times of my life, and hardly anyone recognized that. I looked just the same as everyone else my age; I no longer looked anorexic, but I still felt anorexic. I was just in a bigger body, which I didn't want to be in. Thankfully the therapy and support I'd received and continued to receive helped me see my life and myself differently, but it was very hard to begin with and my recovery grew slowly with time and with a lot of support and encouragement from my family and from the professionals helping me."

I wished we'd been better prepared for this because it all seemed pretty hopeless to us at the time. She'd been ill for two years before getting to the unit and was there for five months, so we were so longing for her recovery. We'd placed our hope on weight restoration being the answer – the cure – and then we discovered it wasn't. That was terribly hard for us, especially as all our friends and family expected her to be back to normal now. We had no knowledge about recovery and the progress that could still come, progress that did indeed come slowly and with time.

We noticed changes in attitude, not just towards food – although of course it was a joy to hear her say "I'm hungry" one day. No, it was more in confidence and in focus that we noticed small things to begin with. She wasn't so introspective, or quite so bound up in worries, or so gloomy. She accepted an invitation to the cinema, which she wouldn't have done before, and apparently shared a bit of popcorn with her friend. It was hard work motivating her and encouraging her, but of course we did; we saw that as our principal role – that and keeping mealtimes, food, and eating as normal and habitual as ever.

We saw progress and a more normal attitude towards life before we saw her think better of her body. She accepted dinner invitations without too much concern and began to make some new friends. I suppose it took a further two years for her to gradually gain confidence and be rid of anorexia, even though her weight had stayed on target all that time.

Helen

Check Point

Dealing with recovery:

- The longer one has anorexia, the harder it is to recover, unlike bulimia. Late twentieth-century studies looking at long-term outcomes for anorexia found that, of those still suffering after five years, nearly 70 per cent had recovered a further five years later. But the figures were very different for those who'd had anorexia for ten years: only just over 10 per cent had recovered five years later.[11] Results from a summary of research findings from 2000 to 2010 for anorexia nervosa and bulimia nervosa generally agree that the outcomes for anorexia are worse than those for bulimia. This is in terms of remission rates ten years or more after the illness. For those with anorexia, 50 per cent are shown to recover and for those with bulimia, 75 per cent.[12]

? How can we help her recover?

Once again an answer to this question is anxiously sought both by parents of younger children living at home and by parents of sons and daughters who are adults. There's a lot you can do – even if it's subtle – and there are things to beware of.

Many clinicians agree that the role of parents is vital – usually a mixture of guidance and support. How much you can guide will depend on the age of your child, your relationship with them, and how entrenched their eating disorder has become, together with their ability and willingness to understand recovery and work towards it. You may be able to help them to discover the cause of their illness and guide them towards seeking professional help, or you may help them to undertake treatment – to "stick with" therapy even though they may be tempted to pull out. Your support will involve giving sustained, unconditional love, encouragement, and constant belief in them, as well as practical acts of caring such as driving them to appointments and nursing them when necessary.

PARENT TO PARENT

My daughter was twenty-seven when her eating disorder began. She had been given a promotion at work and was very nervous about managing such a senior position. I worried that she wasn't sleeping well or eating enough, but of course she reassured me that she was OK and didn't have a problem. Inevitably the weight loss continued and she looked dreadful, she was cold all the time, and her complexion worsened. I had concerns and voiced some of them, but it didn't make her change. I spoke to her husband in confidence and he assured me he was keeping a watchful eye on her. His father rang me rather accusingly, saying, "Did you know she had anorexia?" but didn't offer any thoughts on how we could help her recover.

All that was left for me was to keep supporting her emotionally, which I was able to do as we were very close. I encouraged her to tell me all the difficulties she was experiencing at work and we'd spend the day together each Saturday as her husband worked. That gave me the opportunity to provide lunch for her and to eat as normal together. My father had been a chef and we all liked our food, so talking recipes and trying new things used to be something we'd do. I had to tread very carefully during conversations about food when she was ill, and although I was sick with worry, I tried not to express it to her. She lost around three stone and three dress sizes but I decided not to tell her how ghastly she looked. I tried to build up her confidence by being there for her, and fortunately she did ring me a lot and saw me each weekend.

She saw her doctor because her periods had stopped and I hoped they'd talk about her weight loss, but as far as I'm aware that didn't happen. She didn't receive any professional treatment and remained very thin and unhappy. One dreadful morning, her husband left her. I supported her through the worst emotional upset and of course I worried even more about her health because she was now not eating at all. She couldn't keep anything down, surviving on alcohol alone. She was in a terrible state and off work so I suggested a holiday which, thankfully, she accepted. It was just a week in the sun and a lot of the time she just cried or we talked about things. We always took our meals together and she managed a little something each time.

In many ways the disaster had a positive effect. Her father reminded her that she needed to keep her career now that she was single. She told me that the holiday had put distance between the past and the present and that she was going to focus on her health and get it back; and that was the turning point. She said that the stability and support that I provided were calming and utterly dependable and that she knew she was loved and all this helped her to work on eating again. She said I'd acted as an unpaid counsellor as well as the mum who knew her best.

Patricia

Check Point

Dealing with recovery:

- Each individual deals with recovery in their own way and the path towards recovery varies because of many factors.

- Setbacks are a part of recovery. Serious setbacks or relapses do not necessarily put someone back to the starting point, but can be useful tools for further recovery.

- Many sufferers doubt that full recovery is possible for a number of reasons; therefore it is vital that you believe in recovery and hold that belief for them while you support and encourage them.

? Is there anything we should avoid doing or saying?

Supporting someone who is in the early stages of recovery often involves hearing them battling with their conflicting feelings and taking a very negative view of their own recovery. Unless you are prepared for this it can be extremely distressing, and cause you to despair and react inappropriately.

The supporting role also becomes a very protective one during the period of your child's illness, and an understandable protectiveness can remain while they are attempting to achieve independence from the eating disorder. Therefore, if we're not careful, our children may feel smothered and find it hard to learn to break their dependence on us. It can be very hard to know when to let go a little and when to step in for them, but hopefully you will find that you need to step in less as you child is allowed to make progress. We purposely tried to give our daughter "space" to discuss a feeling or a reaction and we found that she began to make decisions without agonizing or taking forever. We gently encouraged and supported her in learning to cope with eating out and at friends' houses. We noticed that she was happy to go swimming again with the family or with a friend for fun rather than just for exercise, but chose not to comment and draw attention to her or the situation.

Every case will be different, but maybe my further recollections of my daughter learning to make choices for herself and being allowed a little freedom to try living life normally will give you some ideas.

PARENT TO PARENT

I remember when our daughter was discharged from an inpatient unit, where she had spent three months, she said she would stay on the regime until she was eighteen and then she would starve herself again. It really frightened me and obviously upset me, but it wasn't what actually happened – it was more that she was airing her inner conflict. As she remained on the prescribed eating plan and became used to it, her mindset began to change. I had to stay positive and focused whilst at the same time tactful and "laid back" on the surface.

My daughter's psychotherapist encouraged me to go along with her pace of recovery rather than try to dictate it by my own enthusiasm and desire for her to get better. To begin with she was very sensitive to people commenting on how well she looked because she thought that they meant fatter or better, neither of which was acceptable to her at the time. Friends and family members were warned not to greet her in that way.

I was aware that her illness had brought great suffering to her, which needed recognizing, a bit like grief. I also saw that she was not ready to have people think it was all over and forgotten (which many people did, since her weight had been restored and she looked "back to normal"). Allowing her "space", to vent her feelings, and understanding her and loving her through the rages were very important to her recovery. So too was keeping her focused and occupied.

Looking back, some of her first steps towards recovery included a lessening of the emotional outbursts (first in scale and then in frequency); laughing again with her sisters; sitting down with us (many people with anorexia won't sit down as they believe standing up uses more calories) and watching television again; having a bath rather than a shower for the first time in seven months and not being upset looking at her body; saying "I'm hungry"; and being *able to accept a chocolate offered from the box in company. Many of the milestones passed without comment because she didn't like being praised and because it drew attention to normal things that she preferred to ease into without fuss and attention. We had to learn when to comment or praise and when to note them privately and stay silent.*

We were careful to take the lead from her and reserve encouragement for the longer "heart to hearts" or when it seemed appropriate. Needless to say, we got it wrong sometimes and the period was not without some door slamming and shouting.

Jane

ACTION PLAN

Going through to recovery

- Remember that recovery is achievable. Hold on to this, even though present circumstances may seem to deny it.

- Encourage your child to realize that the eating disorder may appear to be the solution for them, but it is actually also the problem they need to get rid of.

- Recovery from an eating disorder is more complicated than from a physical illness, so find out and try to understand what recovery is all about.

- Think of recovery as a journey and a process – it has forward steps, but also some backward ones at times. Just concentrating on regaining a healthy weight or stopping purging is not the whole focus of recovery.

- Look at their motivation for recovery. Help them decide why they want to overcome the eating disorder and keep reminding them.

- Help them set realistic targets and goals for themselves. Advise them not to try to do it all in one step.

- Don't let setbacks get you or them down. They are part of the recovery process – in fact many recovered sufferers admit they learned from setbacks, so prepare for them and use them towards recovery.

- Keep your child focused and purposeful. Talk together about the future and keep them positive.

- Allow them space (within reason and with boundaries) to make changes, and inevitably some mistakes, as a basis for learning and trying again.

- Listen to your child and go along with their pace of recovery.

- Encourage them to keep a diary/notebook of feelings, including both good and bad, and a "Good Things" book or section of their diary where their own attitudes on the positive things about their life can be recorded.

CHAPTER 9

Living Life Free from an Eating Disorder

Living life free from an eating disorder is achievable. At ABC we hear from people who have been recovered for decades, some of whom we have supported. For me and for my daughters, sustained recovery is based primarily on their courage, their determination to be well and to live a good, full, and happy life again, and about the professional support they've been given in treatment. Judging from what they say, it's also about the love and support they've received from their family and a few close friends. But most importantly, it's about their learning to know themselves and their vulnerable times, to take small risks in life, to grow as people and recognize their personal achievements, and to survive all the bad times – the incredibly bad times. I am so proud of them.

Neither of my daughters started her periods for years, and anorexia threatened their fertility as well as their hearts in the long term. They were both seriously at risk of losing their lives and yet they survived and recovered. Their periods did start once they were on the path to recovery and at a good weight (even though this was late at sixteen years old); of course we'd worried that they wouldn't start at all. They have had many scans and tests over the years and have had to learn to live with the adjustment to their bodies during the run up to their monthly periods: the feelings of being bloated; the fluctuation in their weight; the mood swings; and the craving for chocolate. To begin with, they needed particular support from me at this time of the month. Now they ride it like everybody else and enjoy the chocolate without a return to fearing weight gain or bingeing.

Watching out for the vulnerable times

Vulnerable times can sometimes be serious for recovering sufferers and can threaten their freedom. A vulnerable time can be caused by major illness within the family. This was the case for us and first occurred when my daughter had only just left the inpatient clinic following three months of treatment. We found that the trauma caused to our family by her illness (and also a genetic predisposition to eating disorders) resulted in her sister beginning to lose weight owing to extreme anxiety.

Despite her receiving counselling and all our attempts to help, it became a serious problem. We couldn't believe that an eating disorder might be happening again, but exactly two years later we were in the same hospital room with a different daughter. This did, of course, threaten the progress of our recovering daughter greatly, and the professionals told us that she'd never recover. But she didn't slip back, and although there were some very wobbly times, she progressed – in fact they both did – partly because of their determination to be free of the eating disorder, and partly because of our continuous belief in and support for them.

I advise parents to look out for vulnerable times. These are often periods of great stress such as exams, starting a new job, going to college or university; relationship difficulties such as splitting up with a boyfriend, girlfriend, or partner; or body changes such as weight gain during pregnancy. We have seen quite a few of these and although in the earlier days of recovery they did tempt my daughters to revisit some old and damaging coping practices, they managed to resist. Emotional upset from losing a close relative often creates a very vulnerable time. In our case we lost both our closest family friend and a wonderful grandma, who had given us all so much love and support through our lives and the years of illness, so this was a very hard time indeed.

Comfortable with who they are

Then there is the subject of dieting. Did I forbid my daughters to mention the word or to contemplate it ever? Yes, of course, it was one of my greatest fears. But now that we have the years of recovery behind us I can see that my daughters do, like most girls, talk of dieting a bit for the summer bikini or their wedding dress. I can see that they may want to lose some of the baby weight they'll gain after pregnancy and will sometimes unintentionally lose weight during times of stress, illness, or impoverished and forgetful student living. The difference is that they are comfortable with who they are now and tell me they will never risk the life they have with all its opportunities. I now believe them, though I'll always be watchful.

Here's what one of my daughters wrote:

"I think true recovery is being completely free from the power of an eating disorder and the power that it holds over your life. It is possible to achieve recovery, but it can often be a long and difficult journey. I think this is where some people can give up. It is understandable why some feel recovery may only be a far-away hope, but determination is one of the key points to living life free. Being a perfectionist can mean that it is hard to accept setbacks and I often thought I had failed and it was hopeless trying to carry on. I also compared myself to my sister, who recovered relatively quickly, so I felt at a disadvantage. The truth is that everybody's recovery is different and personal to them and setbacks are normal and helpful in understanding how to move forward.

The more pressure I put on myself to recover, the more anxious I became and the more difficult it was to break old habits. Therefore, it's important to believe in yourself and to recognise that the way you talk to yourself and encourage yourself is vital; you need to believe that what you are doing is for you and for your future happiness and wellbeing. However, the support of family and friends is also paramount and was a major aid in my recovery. While parents in particular are usually understandably anxious at letting their child 'loose' into the recovery stage, it is necessary that they have some freedom.

A lot of my friends who were in recovery had parents who were strict up to the point of being suffocating with them, and I really believe their progress was hindered because of it. Parents have to allow their children to venture out for themselves and take a few risks, as well as keeping a watchful eye on them. How can one ever learn to be free without being let go of? I was very lucky in this respect and I remember being allowed to try recovery and find out for myself what freedom felt like.

An eating disorder can feel like a prison where everything is ordered and controlled. Recovery is not meant to be the stark opposite of this and I think that's what people find scary. Recovery is a grey stage, where there is control and rules, but also a chance to kick them off once in a while and experience something different and liberating. It is almost as if you are riding a bike, but being held at the same time. Sometimes you are let go of and can ride on your own; at other times you need the support of the person holding you. Sometimes you fall off, but then get back up and try again.

It is important to pace yourself and to remember that there is safety in recovery, but that this place of safety is real and good, unlike the façade of security that an eating disorder provides. Even when you have recovered and are riding solo, there are times in your life when you need support and knowing this is part of the process. Understanding yourself and your vulnerable times is crucial. Don't be afraid to ask for help or to say that you are struggling.

It is possible to live a life free from the fear that an eating disorder brings, but there will be times when you may struggle or have difficulties, as everyone does in life. The important thing is to recognize and accept that recovery isn't perfect. For me, being recovered is about living life to the full and not being afraid of challenges. It's about eating too much sometimes and not feeling hungry the next; trying new things and taking a few risks; being out of your safe zone and feeling proud and liberated; forgetting the former shadow of yourself and re-inventing a new identity; not being defined by an eating disorder; eating out and enjoying food and drink; and looking forward to the next meal and not feeling guilty. These haven't all come at once to me – it's taken time and I still have difficult days, but I am there now. It's taken dedication, hard work, support, backwards steps, tears, challenges, fear, friendship, and perseverance, but it's been so worth it. Everyone can achieve recovery and no one is bound to an eating disorder, whatever anyone might say. As the poem says, 'Your life is your life; know it while you have it.'[13]*

For me personally, my family was a lifeline during my recovery. Not only was I loved and supported emotionally, but encouraged and listened to. I felt no pressure to recover and whenever setbacks occurred I was reassured and encouraged to continue. I would encourage other parents to be firm, but not suffocating, understanding and willing to listen, positive and optimistic, strong and dependable, loving and encouraging. Unconditional love and support is the greatest thing a parent can give."*

Imogen

The Laughing Heart

your life is your life
don't let it be clubbed into dank submission.
be on the watch.
there are ways out.
there is a light somewhere.
it may not be much light but
it beats the darkness.
be on the watch.
the gods will offer you chances.
know them.
take them.
you can't beat death but
you can beat death in life, sometimes.
and the more often you learn to do it,
the more light there will be.
your life is your life.
know it while you have it.
you are marvelous
the gods wait to delight
in you.

Charles Bukowski

Appendix 1

Possible Health Risks

Signs to watch out for	Possible risk
Feeling faint and/or actually fainting if standing up too fast. Poor circulation with cold hands and feet.	Low blood pressure.
Any sustained weight loss and low Body Mass Index (BMI) (especially below 17.5, which puts someone in the anorexic band). BMI is calculated by dividing a person's weight by their height in metres squared. A normal healthy BMI is between 20 and 25.	Failure to grow in height, heart and organ problems, ultimately even heart attacks.
Slower pulse. When the body runs out of fat to use for energy it uses up muscle, including heart muscle, and a slower pulse occurs as the heart conserves energy. A normal pulse is around 80–90 beats per minute.	Chest pains, heart problems, and ultimately even heart attacks.
Getting out of breath more easily (red blood cells carry the oxygen to your muscles so with too few you have to breathe faster to help get more oxygen moved around) and feeling tired or sluggish.	Anaemia (not enough red blood cells in the blood).
Periods fail to begin, become irregular, or stop altogether, although they can start again when weight and eating improve to near normal.	Under-developed reproductive system, risk of polycystic ovaries, and even infertility.
Not eating properly during adolescence means bones aren't strengthened as much as they should be, so when bone strength is lost in older age bones can become too weak. Bone strength can be lost much more quickly if periods stop for too long.	Osteoporosis (brittle bones) and susceptibility to fractures.

Not drinking, or drinking enough, liquids.	Severe dehydration triggers electrolyte or body salt imbalances that can cause cramps, chills, and nausea, as well as putting strain on overworked kidneys and the heart.
Feeling the cold – someone who is underweight will feel the cold more than other people and may struggle to get warm – even in the height of summer.	Burns can occur, as children stay too close to radiators, use hot water bottles that are far too hot, or take baths in scalding water. A fine down of hair called lanugo can grow over the body to try to keep it warm. Chilblains and circulation problems with hands and feet.
Difficulty sleeping – caused by being underweight or hungry.	Tiredness, exhaustion, depression. Poor concentration by day, restlessness and wandering about at night.
Electrolyte imbalance – when someone makes themselves sick or takes too many laxatives, a lot of water is lost in which are vital chemicals called electrolytes. The balance of these chemicals in the body is essential for keeping the heart beating regularly, as well as for the normal function of the brain.	Electrolyte loss can cause symptoms as serious as heart failure or fits.
Self-induced vomiting.	Weakening of the natural valve at the top of the stomach, causing acid to leak up leading to heartburn and indigestion. Swollen salivary glands below the ears. Rupturing of the stomach and choking on things used to make themselves sick.
Laxative abuse.	Constipation and diarrhoea caused by upsets of the natural rhythm of the bowel. Over time more serious problems like IBS or food intolerances may develop.

Signs to watch out for	Possible risk
Eating too much unhealthy food over a long period.	Changes to the blood vessels in the body.
	Symptoms might not be noticed immediately, but fatty deposits accumulate and can block the vessels and can lead to angina, strokes, and ultimately heart attacks.
Eating too many sugary foods over a long period.	Diabetes. This can cause serious health problems and is linked with heart disease.
Being overweight and eating an unhealthy diet.	An increased risk of all kinds of health problems including many cancers.
	Joint problems such as arthritis linked to being overweight, and joint aches and pains.

Appendix 2

Diagnostic Criteria for Eating Disorders

American Psychiatric Association, *Diagnostic and Statistical Manual of Mental Disorders*, *(DSM-IV-TR)*, fourth edition, text revision, Washington DC: American Psychiatric Association, 2000, 589, 594–95.

There are two specific diagnoses in the DSM-IV-TR: anorexia nervosa and bulimia nervosa, and "an Eating Disorder Not Otherwise Specified (EDNOS) category is also provided for coding disorders that do not meet criteria for a specific Eating Disorder."

Diagnostic Criteria for Anorexia Nervosa

- Refusal to maintain body weight at or above a minimally normal weight for age and height (e.g., weight loss leading to maintenance of body weight less than 85% of that expected; or failure to make expected weight gain during period of growth, leading to body weight less than 85% of that expected).
- Intense fear of gaining weight or becoming fat, even though underweight.
- Disturbance in the way in which one's body weight or shape is experienced, undue influence of body weight or shape on self-evaluation, or denial of the seriousness of the current low body weight.
- In postmenarcheal females, amenorrhea, i.e., the absence of at least three consecutive menstrual cycles. (A woman is considered to have amenorrhea if her periods occur only following hormone, e.g., estrogen, administration.)

Specify type:

Restricting type: during the current episode of Anorexia Nervosa, the person has not regularly engaged in binge-eating or purging behaviour (i.e., self-induced vomiting or the misuse of laxatives, diuretics, or enemas).

Binge–Eating/Purging Type: during the current episode of Anorexia Nervosa, the person has regularly engaged in binge-eating or purging behaviour (i.e., self-induced vomiting or the misuse of laxatives, diuretics, or enemas).

Diagnostic Criteria for Bulimia Nervosa

- Recurrent episodes of binge eating. An episode of binge eating is characterized by both of the following:
- » Eating, in a discrete period of time (e.g., within any 2 hour period), an amount of food that is definitely larger than most people would eat during a similar period of time and under similar circumstances.
- » A sense of lack of control over eating during the episode (e.g., a feeling that one cannot stop eating or control what or how much one is eating).
- Recurrent inappropriate compensatory behaviour in order to prevent weight gain, such as self-induced vomiting; misuse of laxatives, diuretics, enemas, or other medications; fasting; or excessive exercise.
- The binge eating and inappropriate compensatory behaviours both occur, on average, at least twice a week for 3 months.
- Self-evaluation is unduly influenced by body shape and weight.
- The disturbance does not occur exclusively during episodes of Anorexia Nervosa.

Specify type:

Purging Type: during the current episode of Bulimia Nervosa, the person has regularly engaged in self-induced vomiting or the misuse of laxatives, diuretics, or enemas.

Nonpurging Type: during the current episode of Bulimia Nervosa, the person has used other inappropriate compensatory behaviours, such as fasting or excessive exercise, but has not regularly engaged in self-induced vomiting or the misuse of laxatives, diuretics, or enemas.

Eating Disorder Not Otherwise Specified

The Eating Disorder Not Otherwise Specified category is for disorders of eating that do not meet the criteria for any specific Eating Disorder. Examples include:

- For females, all of the criteria for Anorexia Nervosa are met except that the individual has regular menses.
- All of the criteria for Anorexia Nervosa are met except that, despite significant weight loss, the individual's current weight is in the normal range.
- All of the criteria for Bulimia Nervosa are met except that the binge eating and inappropriate compensatory mechanisms occur at a frequency of less than twice a week or for a duration of less than 3 months.
- The regular use of inappropriate compensatory behaviour by an individual of normal body weight after eating small amounts of food (e.g., self-induced vomiting after the consumption of two cookies).
- Repeatedly chewing and spitting out, but not swallowing, large amounts of food.
- Binge-eating disorder: recurrent episodes of binge eating in the absence of the regular use of inappropriate compensatory behaviours characteristic of Bulimia Nervosa.

Notes

1. Cognitive Behavioural Therapy (CBT) is the NHS's preferred option for psychotherapy used in counselling, but not everyone responds well to this form of therapy. There are many alternative forms of "talking therapy" such as Cognitive Analytic Therapy, hypnotherapy, and Neuro-linguistic Programming (NLP), person-centred counselling, and so on. Expressive forms of therapy involving art, music, poetry, etc. can also be very valuable.

2. Refer to ABC's contact details in the Useful Contacts section of this book.

3. Periods can stop when a girl is only about 80 to 85 per cent of her normal weight for her age and height. They can resume once a girl is 95 to 98 per cent of her normal weight for her age and height.

4. See Keys, A., Brozek, J., Henschel, A., Mickelsen, O., and Taylor, H. L., *The Biology of Human Starvation*.

5. NICE guidelines advise, "4.2.3 There can be serious long-term consequences to a delay in obtaining treatment. 4.2.3.1 People with eating disorders should be assessed and receive treatment at the earliest opportunity."

6. Dawson, Dee, *Anorexia and Bulimia: A Parents' Guide to Recognising Eating Disorders and Taking Control*, page 114.

7. Visit www.childgrowthfoundation.org

8. Bryant-Waugh, Rachel and Lask, Bryan, *Eating Disorders: A Parents' Guide*, page 98.

9. Obsessive Compulsive Disorder (OCD) is an anxiety disorder characterized by persistent intrusive and seemingly irrational obsessive thoughts to perform repetitive behaviours that interfere with normal living.

10. Nasogastric (tube) feeding can be vital to patients whose weight is extremely low but it should be administered by trained and experienced nursing staff.

11. Strober, M., Freeman, R., and Morrell, W., "The Long-term Course of Severe Anorexia Nervosa in Adolescents: Survival Analysis of Recovery, Relapse, and Outcome Predictors Over 10–15 Years in a Prospective Study", *International Journal of Eating Disorders*, 22:4, 1997, pages 339–360.

12. Keel, Pamela K., and Brown, Tiffany A., "Update on Course and Outcome in Eating Disorders", *International Journal of Eating Disorders*, 43:3, 2010, 195–204, page 202.

13. Bukowski, Charles, *The Laughing Heart*, Santa Rosa: Black Sparrow Press (now HarperCollins/ECCO), 1996.

Suggested Reading

- Bryant-Waugh, Rachel and Lask, Bryan, *Eating Disorders: A Parents' Guide*, London: Penguin Books, 1999 (a 2004 edition published by Routledge is also available).

- Dawson, Dee, *Anorexia and Bulimia: A Parents' Guide to Recognising Eating Disorders and Taking Control*, London: Vermilion, 2001.

- Garner, D. M., reviews A. Keys's work in the chapter "Psychoeducational Principles in the Treatment of Eating Disorders", in Gamer, D. M., and Garfinkel, P. E., eds, *Handbook of Treatment for Eating Disorders*, New York: Guilford Press, 1997, pages 145–77.

- Keys, A., Brozek, J., Henschel, A., Mickelsen, O., and Taylor, H. L., *The Biology of Human Starvation* (2 vols), Minneapolis: University of Minnesota Press, 1950.

- Langley, J. *Boys Get Anorexia Too: Coping with Male Eating Disorders in the Family*, London: Paul Chapman Publishing, London, 2006.

- Treasure, Janet, Smith, Gráinne, and Crane, Anna, *Skills-based Learning for a Loved One with an Eating Disorder*, Hove: Routledge, 2007.

National Institute for Health and Clinical Excellence (NICE)

The National Institute for Clinical Excellence (NICE) is a group working within the UK health system to produce guidelines for the treatment of all kinds of health issues. Working from research findings, it recommends best practice for treatment. Versions are published for medical professionals, patients, and their families.

The NICE eating disorders clinical guidelines (CG9), published in 2004, make recommendations for the identification, treatment, and management of anorexia nervosa, bulimia nervosa, and related eating disorders (in particular binge-eating disorder) in children aged eight years through to adults. They advise on physical and psychological treatments, treatment with medicines, and what kinds of services best help people with eating disorders. However, they do not look at obesity or how to diagnose or treat an eating problem that has been caused by another physical or mental disorder.

NICE guidelines on eating disorders – information for the public (including patients and their carers): http://guidance.nice.org.uk/CG9/PublicInfo/pdf/English

NICE guidelines on eating disorders – quick reference guide: http://guidance.nice.org.uk/CG9/QuickRefGuide/pdf/English
ISBN 978-1-85433 398 4
www.nice.org.uk

published by:
The British Psychological Society,
St Andrews House,
48 Princess Road East,
Leicester,
LE1 7DR
www.bps.org.uk

and

The Royal College of Psychiatrists,
17 Belgrave Square,
London,
SW1X 8PG
www.rcpsych.ac.uk

Useful Contacts

Anorexia and Bulimia Care (ABC)

A national charity that supports anyone who is suffering because of eating disorders: sufferers, their families, and carers. It also provides advice for professionals.

Parent Support Line: **01934 710 645**

Sufferer Support Line: **01934 710 679**

Website: **www.anorexiabulimiacare.org.uk**

beat (beating eating disorders)

Working name of leading national charity, the Eating Disorders Association, which works to support and provide advice and help for people with eating disorders and their families.

Helpline for people aged 18 and over: **0845 634 1414**

Helpline for those aged 25 and over: **0845 634 7650**

Website: **www.b-eat.co.uk**

(BACP) British Association for Counselling and Psychotherapy

The Client Information Helpdesk enables potential clients to find a suitable counsellor with whom they feel comfortable, in their particular area. They are happy to discuss any queries or concerns which may arise whilst choosing a counsellor or during the counselling process.

Tel: **0145 588 3316**

Website: **www.bacp.co.uk**

Care for the Family

A national charity that aims to promote strong family life and to help those who face family difficulties.

Initiatives include a UK telephone befriending service for parents of children who are receiving treatment for an eating disorder. This offers parents one-to-one, ongoing support from trained 'befrienders' who have been through the experience of seeing their own child struggle with an eating disorder.

Tel: 029 2081 0800

Email: eatingdisorders@cff.org.uk.

Website: www.careforthefamily.co.uk

MIND

The leading mental health charity for England and Wales.

Mindinfoline: 0845 766 0163

Website: www.mind.org.uk

Rethink

Leading national mental health membership charity that works to help those affected by severe mental illness recover a better quality of life. Provides advice about mental illness as well as related issues including legal rights and benefits.

Tel: 0845 456 0455 (Mon–Fri 10 a.m. – 2 p.m.)

Website: www.rethink.org

SANE

Offers emotional support, crisis care, and detailed information to people experiencing mental health problems, their family, carers, health and other professionals.

SANELine: 0845 767 8000 (every day 6 p.m. - 11p.m.)

Website: www.sane.org.uk

The Institute of Psychiatry

The Institute's Eating Disorders Unit provides a range of high-quality services for patients of all ages. A wide range of information, including information for carers can be found on their eating disorders website.

Website: www.iop.kcl.ac.uk/sites/edu

YoungMinds

UK charity committed to improving the emotional wellbeing of children and young people and empowering their parents and helpers.

Parents' helpline: 0808 802 5544

Website: www.youngminds.org.uk